Santa Cruz Is in the Heart

Selected Writings on Local History, Culture, Politics & Ghosts

By Geoffrey Dunn

Capitola Book Company

Earlier versions of the following stories and poems originally appeared in:
Chinquapin, Cruzan, The Express, Good Times, Monterey Life, The News, The Santa Cruz Sentinel, The Sun, Taste, and *Zeitgeist.* "At Twenty-four" is excerpted from an unpublished work entitled *Cargoed Apples.* Photographs have been provided by the following sources: G.L. Alnas, Covello & Covello, Creative Arts Books, Don Fukuda, Gary Lamb, George Lee, George Ow Family Collection, Joan Stagnaro Collection, UCSC Special Collections, Victor Varela, and the private collection of the author.

Cover Photo: Lawrence Zolezzi, "Babe" Stagnaro, and Joe Loero (the author's uncles) at the Santa Cruz Municipal Wharf, c.1945.

Dunn, Geoffrey F.
    Santa Cruz Is in the Heart.
    1. Santa Cruz History . 2. Chinese History in California. 3. Italian
    History in California. 4. Ethnic History in California. 5. Ernest Otto.
I. Title

ISBN Number: 0-932319-02-5

Capitola Book Company

First Printing

Santa Cruz Is in the Heart

For Oryan, Siri and Lindy—
all my love

CONTENTS

For those who pass without entering, the city is one thing; it is another for those who are trapped by it and never leave. There is the city where you arrive for the first time; and there is another city which you leave never to return.

Italo Calvino,
Invisible Cities

Upon the amusement pier I watch
The creeping darkness gather in the west.
Above the giant funhouse and the ghosts
I hear the seagulls call. They're going west
Toward some great Catalina of a dream
Out where the poem ends.
                    But does it end?
The birds are still in flight. Believe the birds.

Jack Spicer,
Collected Poems

INTRODUCTION

ONE OF MY FIRST JOBS as a kid was folding newspapers for a nickel a roll in an old storage shed on the Santa Cruz Municipal Wharf. It was in the early 1960s. My mother's family ran a fishmarket back then, and they used the newspaper as a wrap for the various sea foods which they sold to their customers. From time to time I would peek my head out from the shed (filled with ropes and nets and the smell of the sea) and watch the scene unfolding before me. And what a scene! Scores of Italian fishermen, whose boats were still kept year-round on the wharf, were ablaze with energy as they mended their nets, cut bait, and argued vociferously among themselves. Still other visitors to the wharf—Filipinos, Portuguese, Chinese, Japanese, Blacks and Anglos—came down to buy or catch their evening meal. Who knows how long I would stand there taking it all in, grinning, no doubt, at the colorful daily drama unfolding before me? Soon enough, one of my uncles would fling a fish head in my vicinity, indicating that it was time to get back to work. I fell in love with Santa Cruz then. And I have been in love ever since.

Not long ago, a local magazine ran a regular column entitled "Why I Live in Santa Cruz." In essence, the guest columnists were writing about their love affairs with the city. For the most part, they waxed poetic about Santa Cruz's natural beauties—its mountains and beaches, its parks and vistas, and the wonders of Monterey Bay. Or they wrote about the city's restaurants and movie houses, its temperate climate and architecture, and at least one person, I seem to recall, wrote about its "softness of light." They were all right, of course; Santa Cruz is one of the most beautiful places on earth. There is no other place quite like it.

For me, however, the physical beauties of Santa Cruz have always been secondary perks. What holds me here is the spirit of the place—the spirit of its people—of both those who have lived here before us and those who live here now. This place has always had a special human feel to it, and anyone who would deny it had better check again.

This book is thus a collection of short writings of mine, completed during the last decade, which attempt to illuminate the heart and spirit of Santa Cruz—and which, I hope, sound an alarm in some areas where I feel they are presently threatened. Diverse as these pieces are in style, theme and time frame, they share, I feel, a common sensitivity and vision, and an unyielding belief in the power of the heart.

While each story, essay or poem stands by itself, I have attempted to organize them loosely in respect to chronology. This is not, however, a comprehensive history of Santa Cruz, and not all of the pieces collected herein fall into a neat chronological time slot. The story on the Ow family, for instance, begins in 1947, cuts back to the 1880s, then slowly meanders back to the present. Other stories follow similar paths. The placement of each story in the text, therefore, is only a general indication of what time period it may begin—and where it might end.

Virtually all of the pieces collected here first appeared in other regional publications, and their original date of publication appears at the end of each piece. I have edited them slightly (and in some cases, substantially) to maintain stylistic continuity and to avoid duplication, but in some cases, eliminating repetition was impossible. You will, for example, read more than once about the anti-Chinese movement of the late Nineteenth Century. So be it. Some things should not be forgotten.

Included here are over two-dozen pieces, many of which are personal, others less so. I've left out some stories which others might have included and have included some which others might have given to my uncles for fish wrap. My final criterion for including a selection was whether or not it provided a unique glimpse (however small) of day-to-day life in our community. It is my judgment—and mine alone—that they have met this test.

One story that I wrangled over including is the piece entitled "Climbing Golden Mountain." It was originally published in the Santa Cruz *Express* in the fall of 1983, well before I met Cabrillo College instructor Sandy Lydon or knew that he was working on a grand treatise about the Monterey Bay Chinese. We had, of course, covered a great deal of the same historic terrain in our research, and I was often told that I was following in his footsteps; undaunted, I persisted with my research and published the story anyway.

With the appearance of *Chinese Gold* two years later, Lydon provided us with the most thorough historical account of Monterey Bay history—Chinese or otherwise—ever written. Quite honestly, there is little in "Climbing Golden Mountain" that does not appear in *Chinese Gold*. Nonetheless, I have decided to include the piece not only because it differs somewhat in interpretation from *Chinese Gold* (which it does), but also because it serves as a good introduction to local Chinese history and may well inspire even more readers to open Lydon's informative book.

Unlike many social scientists, I do not believe that history is merely a series of dates, facts and figures to be interwoven by complex theories, nor do I believe it should be written about that way. History is made by people—quite often not as they please, as Karl Marx reminded us—but real, breathing, working, emotional human beings nonetheless. That is why I have tried to infuse the historical pieces in *Santa Cruz Is in the Heart* with as much humanity as possible. Thus, the title piece of this collection (which is, incidentally, derived from Carlos Bulosan's classic work *America Is in the Heart*) focuses on the life of one man—my dear friend, Freddy Alnas—while at the same time telling the history of Filipinos in Santa Cruz County. It is my belief that by knowing Freddy better you will also know Filipino-American history better, but I will leave that up to the book's readers to decide.

Given that these stories were originally published in popular journals, I have not included footnotes. In my historical pieces, I have oftentimes cited the specific source in the text itself. Generally, the background sources for my historical works have been early-day Santa Cruz newspapers, the *Sentinel,* *Surf,* and *Courier-Item.* I have spent many long hours during the last two decades pouring over their microfilm in the Santa Cruz Public Library. Since 1986 this task has been made considerably easier by indexes of both the *Sentinel* (1856-1884) and the *Surf* (1883-1900) compiled by "Friends of the Library" and which are now available at the Branciforte and Central branches of the Santa Cruz Public Library system. Leon Rowland's *Santa Cruz: The Early Years* has also been a rich source of background material, and, since 1985, so has Lydon's *Chinese Gold.* I have also consulted from time to time *A Sidewalk Companion to Santa Cruz Architecture* by John Chase and Margaret Koch's *Santa Cruz County: Parade of the Past.* Collections of historical writings by Ernest Otto located in the Santa Cruz Public Library, Special Collections at UC Santa Cruz, and the private collection of Lillian McPherson Rouse have also provided a wealth of important historical information. A book long out of print, Henry A.V.C. Torchianas' *Story of the Mission Santa Cruz*, which I recently stumbled across in the stacks of the Cabrillo College Library, contains a multitude of information about early Santa Cruz, and was used as a background source for the opening chapter, "The Confessions of Old Chepa." So, too, was the magnificent book by Malcolm Margolin, *The Ohlone Way*.

In addition to *Chinese Gold* and a series of unpublished interviews with the Ow family conducted by Lydon and Nikki Silva, my chapter on the Ows was greatly enhanced by two private manuscripts, "Grandpa and the Golden Mountain," by George Ow, Jr., and a story by Karin Yien about her grandmother Gue She Lee. An oral history of my great-uncle, Malio Stagnaro, conducted by Elizabeth Calciano and available at both the Santa Cruz Public Library and at UCSC's Special Collections, served as a rich and colorful background source for many of the stories. Paul Stubbs and Carol Champion of UCSC's Special Collections have also been helpful over the years in tracking down various resource materials.

For the most part, however, the primary sources for these stories have been interviews—both formal and informal—with people who have lived much of their lives in Santa Cruz: Freddy Alnas, Don Yee, Victor Ghio, Helen Weston, Anna Liu, George Lee, and many others. If there is any vitality in these stories, it is because of them. My gratitude is expressed by the care and work that went into each chapter.

Which leads me to the final, and for me, at least, the most important section of this introduction. This past summer I read a book by an academic historian who noted how much he detested long lists of acknowledgements at the beginning of books. I suppose it would be nice for writers to pretend that they did all of their work on their own, that they operated in some sort of social and emotional vacuum, but in the case of this book, at least, it would be an outright deception. And while it would be impossible to list all of the people who have in some way contributed to the completion of this book, it is with considerable gratitude that I make the following acknowledgements.

Writing can often be the loneliest of professions. For the most part, you sit by yourself in a room, placing pen to paper in quiet, tedious solitude. The walls close in on you and time seems to stand still. In all honesty, the very nature of the labor goes against my grain. Fortunately, Santa Cruz has a large and thriving community of writers who must daily pass through the same tribulations, and their supportive companionship over the years has helped me through the frustrations inherent to the trade. They include: Greg Beebe, Bruce Bratton, Pat Burnson, Rose Dean, Jim DuGuid, Diana Hembree, Rick Hildreth, Jeanne Wakatsuki Houston, Jim Houston, Bob Johnson, Elizabeth Kadetsky, Guy Lasnier, Sandy Lydon, Morton Marcus, Chris Matthews, Barbara McKenna, Dean Metcalf, Sam Mitchell, Tai Moses, Marshall Motz, Davia Nelson, Elizabeth Schilling, Nikki Silva, Roz Spafford, Christina Waters, Cliff Welch, and Carter Wilson. My editors throughout the years have also been most helpful. They include: Chris Bessler, Buzz Bezore, George Fuller, Michael S. Gant, Stephen Kessler, Kevin Samson, Sheila Schmitz and Harry Stoll. Were it not for their belief in my writing and their steady encouragement, the pieces collected here would never have seen the light of day.

In addition to my written work, I have also spent a good part of the last five years toiling on a series of documentary and feature films. In many cases my film and writing endeavors have overlapped. Once again, I have received the support and assistance from a number of members of the local film and video communities who, in something of a roundabout way, have also contributed to this book. They include: Bill Ackridge, Greg Becker, Harrod Blank, Rick Chatenever, Romney Dunbar, Fast Edy, Tony Hill, Cori Houston, Dirk Martin, Bonita Mugnani, Rito Padilla, Nancy Raney, John Sandidge, and Jon Silver. My partner at Gold Mountain Productions for the last half decade, Mark Schwartz, has been a friend, critic, sounding board and therapist—and he has consistently helped to make me a better writer. My thanks.

After living in Santa Cruz now for over three decades, I have had the good fortune to make many other friends throughout the years—classmates, teachers, teammates, co-workers, colleagues and drinking partners. Their hearts have also made their way into these pages: Dennis Albaugh, Al Barabas, Phil Baldwin, Frank Bardacke, Violet Battistini, Wendy Baxter, Linda Bergthold, Bob Bishop, Dan Butera, Tony Calcagno, Dante "California" Canepa, Frank and Joe Cardinale, Jancy Chang, Chester Charlton, Larry Chew, Jack and Luella Lee Churchill, Francis Corr, Susan Curtis, Tom Curtiss, Bill Domhoff, Ben Dunn, Marge Frantz, Hardy Frye, Don Fukuda, Jeff Genovese, Sue Gin; the Hamm, Meyer and Stewart brothers; Bristow Hardin, Rip Harris, Andy Hernandez, Ken Hiobb, Tim Jenkins, Bob Lee, Bob Lissner, Ari Marcus, John McCuen, Rick Moran, Chris Moore, Ed Morrison, Rex Nicolaisen, David Ow, the Pate and Poen families, Sherry Phillips, Garry Rollison, Nikki Silva, Sue Stolle, Arthur Swanson, Jeff Sweet, David Traxel, Jim Umland; Cullyn, Jerry, Patrice and Rory Vaeth; Mark Wagner, Ron Walters, Ruth Warren, Liza Weiman, David Wellman, Darryl Whitemeyer and Mardi Wormhoudt. The late Steve "Hugo" Larson, Robby Canepa, Skip Littlefield, Garson Matosoff, Wayne Sturtevant, and Alice Swanson, all of whose presences I truly miss, but whose spirits are with me always, have also had a hand in this book. Robert Poen and Claire Rubach have both been the very best of friends throughout the years and have seen me through many a dark hour. Most of these stories were written while I basked in the warmth of their friendship. Without them, quite simply, they would not have been written.

To those who I have forgotten in this mad rush to meet a deadline, please forgive me.

As many of the following stories will attest, my family is—and always has been—a central part of my life. My uncle

Robert Stagnaro, my aunts Gilda Stagnaro and Betty Lamb have looked out for me since childhood (no easy task), and to them my heartfelt thanks. Many of my family members have passed away in recent years—my great-uncle Malio Stagnaro, my uncles Joe and "Stago" Stagnaro, my aunts Estrella and Joan Stagnaro and Mary Herman, and far too many more— and the pain I feel from the missing is compensated only by the strength of their love and spirit while they were here. To my sister, Peggy Dunn, my brother-in-law, Gary Judd, my cousins Kenneth Lamb; Bill, Cottardo, Doug and Malio Stagnaro, and to my many other aunts, uncles, cousins and assorted relatives, my love and thanks.

This book itself is the by-product of long hours of work by a number of people. Beverly Stevens of Accu-riter typed my original manuscript and made many helpful editorial suggestions. Genevieve Heth designed the book's cover, while Chris Meek of Document Design and Data designed and produced the book's text. Chris Moore and Julia Jacobson dutifully proofed the galleys and corrected many editorial errors. And most importantly, my friend, George Ow, Jr., of the Capitola Book Company believed in the project enough to publish the book. His support over the years—not only of me, but of numerous other artists in the community—has made Santa Cruz a better place to live for all of us.

And finally, a note of eternal gratitude to the three people to whom this book is dedicated. They are the heart of the Santa Cruz I love.

Geoffrey Dunn
January, 1989

Santa Cruz Is in the Heart

THE CONFESSIONS OF OLD CHEPA:
Josefa Pérez Soto and the Spirit of Old Santa Cruz

*Listen to me, **mi hijo**, I have a story to tell. The spirits of the wind and the sun are singing to me, **hijo**, and the coyote spirit is dancing. Oh, such a joyous world, but now, it lives only in my heart.*

*It is getting late, **mi hijo**, and I have such a long story to tell. It is the story of Santa Cruz before the **extranjeros**—the people of the mule spirit—came. Such a sacred place, this land of rivers, mountains and the sea.*

*I am an old woman, **mi hijo**, with skin of leather and breath of fire, but I am also very wise. Over eighty summers I have seen. The people of the town laugh at me now and the little children call me names. They do not see the spirit of the coyote dancing on my shoulder. We are dancing on the brink of the world, **mi hijo**, do not laugh at me. Such a long story to tell.*

3

The year is 1889. On the sloping eastside banks of the San Lorenzo River, near the juncture of Branciforte and Water Streets, an old woman with a cane and satchel is beginning her daily journey through Santa Cruz. She is dressed in a tattered green wool sweater, a faded full-length skirt and leather sandals. Around her head is a red bandanna, holding back her long, grey strands of hair. Her eyes are as dark as polished ebony, and her skin is as rough as the bark of an oak. It is mid-morning as she descends the path to the footbridge which crosses the San Lorenzo and leads into town.

The old woman's real name is Josefa Pérez Soto, but the people of Santa Cruz call her "Old Chepa" (the "hunched one") or simply "mother." She is as familiar to the towns-people as the summer fog, and she greets each passerby with a friendly, if time-weary, *"Buenos días."*

To see her on her daily journey is to see a woman in dire poverty, bent and shriveled, but the merchants of Pacific Avenue have taken kindly to her plight. Each day they give to her freely meats and vegetables, corn meal and tobacco, and, perhaps, a shot of whiskey. With her satchel full, she makes her way back up the path to her small rustic cabin in the Villa de Branciforte, or what the whites in Santa Cruz call "Spanish Town." There, she rolls her tobacco in small strips of old newspaper and basks in the summer sun on the south side of her cabin. Perhaps one of her grandchildren will visit her, or maybe an old friend. If not, she is content to be alone.

Down the path and across the river, the people of white Santa Cruz tell stories about "Old Chepa" and shake their heads. Many believe her to be an Indian. Little do they know that Josefa Pérez Soto was once the belle of Old Santa Cruz, born into one of its oldest and more prominent Spanish families. In her eighties, if not nineties, she is nearly as old as the city itself—and she has lived here under four flags: those of Spain, Mexico, the California Republic and the United States. In many ways, her life and the history of nineteenth-century Santa Cruz are one and the same.

4

As the sun begins to set over the barren bluffs to the west, Josefa slowly finds her way into her cabin. Soon, a small fire is crackling, and some beans, salted meat and tortillas are ready to eat.

Josefa Pérez Soto was born in the Villa de Branciforte in the early 1800s. Her father, José Maria Pérez, of Spanish and Indian blood, was a native of Jalisco, Mexico, and a soldier in the Spanish army. Her mother, Margarita Rodriguez, was the fifth daughter of José Antonio Rodriguez, a retired Spanish solider who first arrived in Santa Cruz County in 1798.

The Santa Cruz Mission—the mission of the "holy cross"—was founded by Franciscan priests in 1791, the Spanish government granting to the mission vast tracts of land between the Pájaro River and Point Año Nuevo. Six years later, under orders from the Spanish Viceroy in Mexico City, a separate *villa* was established on the eastern banks of the San Lorenzo River, roughly a mile from the mission. A handful of local priests protested the establishment of a secularized settlement so close to their own, but to no avail. On July 24, 1797, the Villa de Branciforte was officially founded.

Never fulfilling its original economic expectations and in need of regular subsidization, the villa stumbled into the Nineteenth Century inhabited by a growing number of *invalidados*, retired Spanish soldiers who had served ten or more years in the Spanish Army. By most accounts they were a coarse lot, prone to drinking and gambling, and content with the easy life that the rich local soils and congenial coastal climate afforded them. The priests at the Santa Cruz Mission, still offended by the presence of the villa, were outraged by the lazy behavior of the nearby *invalidados* and further accused them of coveting the young women at the mission. The tension between the two communities never ceased.

Nonetheless, a handful of the *invalidados* settled down with families and eventually became prosperous. José and Vincenta Rodriguez raised nine children, four of whom were later to receive land grants in the region from the Mexican government. Their eldest daughter, Margarita, married soldier José Maria Pérez, and they, too, settled in Branciforte. Josefa was their first child.

*There were few women in the villa then, **mi hijo**, and when my mother broke water they brought in an old Indian woman from the mission. They had given her the name Jovita. It was she who brought me into this world. She placed water to my mother's lips and stroked her gently with the claw of a grizzly bear. It gave her strength.*

When I was young, Jovita would come to the villa and care for us children when we were sick. Her eyes were like bright stars. She taught me the ways of her people, their dances and chants, their medicines and their holy visions. And the power of the sun.

*As we grew older, we would play in the river. We would wade in up to our knees and look for the brightest pebbles and give them names. The children from the mission, **los inditos**, would join us in the river, and we would play games together with the bright stones and chase the small green frogs in the shallows. I will tell you that they never touched the frogs.*

*I remember the summer that one of them died, and then four more, and then a dozen, and then there were no more. Not even Jovita could save them. That was **el verano de la muerte**, **mi hijo**, the summer of death, and I never played in the river again.*

The mission across the river was a world separate and apart from young Josefa's. Established under the pretext of bringing God and prosperity to the native Ohlone population, the missions, in fact, differed little from the slave system of the American south. The Ohlones at the mission toiled long hours for little personal gain, their labor being expropriated for great wealth which went directly into the hands of the church. By 1830, the Santa Cruz Mission had accumulated over 3,600 head of cattle, 400 horses, large herds of sheep and swine, and $25,000 worth of silver plate.

Later apologists for the Mission would claim (and for that

matter, continue to claim) that the native Ohlone had joined
the church of their own free will, but that was hardly the case.
Years after the mission had collapsed, a local Ohlone was
interviewed about his life in the mission. His Christian name
was Lorenzo, and he told the following tale: "To capture the
wild Indian, first were taken the children, and then the parents
followed. The *padres* would erect a hut, and light the candles
to say mass, and the Indians, attracted by the light—thinking
they were stars—would approach, and soon be taken." Lorenzo
told further stories of "being severely treated by the *padres*."
Lashings with rawhide straps were commonplace.

By the time Mexico declared its independence from Spain
in 1833 and the missions were secularized, the Ohlone population at the Santa Cruz Mission had dropped from a high of 644
in 1798 to 250.

*At night I would be awakened by loud shrieks, **mi hijo**, and at first
I thought that they were coyotes in the fields. But they were not coyotes,
no, and if I listened closely and the wind was blowing from the west, I
could hear the cracks of the whip and the screams of pain that followed.
Oh no, they were not coyotes. Even the little children would receive the
whip, **mi hijo**, smaller than you, and we would see the welts on their
backs as they worked in the fields, their heads held down in shame.*

*One day in the river, before the summer of death, I heard the **inditos**
tell the story of the murdered **padre**, Father Andres Quintana, **el padre
malo**, they called him. It was said he beat his disciples with the iron
whip, tortured them, and that he took advantage of a young married
Ohlone woman. Late one night, when the bad priest was alone, he was
called from his quarters, beaten, then hung from a tree behind the
mission hill. Before he died, those parts that held his manhood were cut
away from his groin. His ghost still hangs from the tree behind the hill,
blood dripping to the soil. All my life, **mi hijo**, I could never go back to
the mission without seeing him, **el padre malo**, swaying there in the
wind.*

By the time she reached adolescence, Josefa Pérez had become a striking beauty and she was given the name "*la más bonita de Santa Cruz.*" It was rumored that the popular song "The Maid of Monterey" was written in her honor.

Immediately following Mexico's declaration of independence from Spain, the newly-established government granted large tracts of land to a handful of selected citizens. In what is now Santa Cruz County, nearly twenty such grants were awarded, three of which went to Josefa's uncles, Francisco, José Antonio, and José de la Cruz Rodriguez and another to her cousin, Blas Escamilla. Together, the family's land holdings constituted thousands of acres, on which they ranched cattle, swine, horses and sheep. They were among the region's most prosperous residents and their monthly rodeos, at which the men branded the cattle and rode wild broncos, were large, gala celebrations where the young and beautiful Josefa was said to be the most sought-after partner for the evening dances.

Oh, I had fire in my eyes back then, mi hijo, and the men would stare, hoping to douse the flame. I could feel the heat of their wanting—my father said you could cut it with a knife—and my body would twist and pull to the rhythms of the music, but I never gave them what they wanted. I never even looked their way—not until I was ready.

In her early twenties, Josefa Pérez was married to Gervasio Soto, the son of a former mission official, and they settled above Powder Mill Flat, near the present site of Paradise Park. During the following decades, Josefa gave birth to seven children, four sons and three daughters.

By the mid-1840s, Santa Cruz was on the precipice of great change. Scores of Anglo settlers began moving into the county, many of them U.S. citizens bearing no loyalty to the government of Mexico.

In the spring of 1840, according to Leon Rowland's *The Annals of Santa Cruz,* José Castro, Prefect of Northern California and a cousin of the Santa Cruz Castro family, ordered that all "*extranjeros,*" or foreigners, be rounded up by local authorities. Such residents were taken to Monterey and placed on a ship to San Blas, Mexico, though within a year many had returned to the region. By the end of the decade, Santa Cruz was a hotbed of secessionist sentiments. With the coming of the Gold Rush, the days of Mexican rule were to be short lived.

In February of 1846, Lieutenant John C. Fremont and his "California Battalion," riding under the flag of the United States on what was then foreign soil, crossed over the Santa Cruz mountains from Santa Clara. According to Fremont's diaries, his party camped for three nights on Thompson Flat (now the Graham Hill Show Grounds), across the river from the Soto family. Famished from their journey through the redwoods, Fremont's soldiers sought to regain their strength on the picturesque bluff overlooking Monterey Bay. Although caught in a torrential downpour, Fremont was able to secure enough supplies to resuscitate his troops. It was said that Josefa Soto brought food to the men, cooked for them, and cared for the sick. Later, she was arrested by Mexican authorities in Santa Clara on charges of being a spy.

*We could hear the soldiers coming across the mountains, the rumble of their horses and the singing. The first day we saw smoke rising from their campground, and then a party of two soldiers forged the river by horseback and arrived at my house. At first they demanded food, but when I denied them, they offered a gold coin in return. I was never to see that coin, **mi hijo**, never. It was late winter and I gathered what supplies I could and mounted the smaller of the two horses behind one of the soldiers. He joked about my womanhood in English to his companion, and though I could not understand the words, **mi hijo**, I understood just the same. They are all alike.*

*When we arrived at the camp, **El Commandante** Fremont approached me and offered me his tent. Question after question he asked, about roads and military supplies, rivers and ships. I pretended I did not understand. I did not trust him, **El Commandante**. His Spanish was very broken. He said he was here merely to make maps. He was a liar. He was here to exploit us. He had the look of death.*

9

And then I was introduced to the troops. Many were sick and weakened from their journey. I could not let them die. I made a broth out of the herbs taught to me by Jovita when I was young, and nearly all were better by the following morning. They asked me to secure young girls from the villa for them, but I refused. I told them that they were not good enough. They laughed, but the truth is, they never were.

On the fourth morning, El Commandante Fremont bid me farewell. Instead of gold, he handed me a small locket of brass. He laughed and made a joke of me and mounted his horse. I threw the locket to the ground.

California was admitted to the union in 1851, and by then, Santa Cruz was swarming with newly-arrived whites on the make. Those *Californios* of Spanish and Mexican heritage who still resided here were called "greasers" by the Anglos, and a new and ugly chapter in Santa Cruz history was about to unfold. For the next three decades, rapes and lynchings of *Californios* would become commonplace. The first such lynchings took place here as soon as California became a state and didn't end until 1877.

The California Census of 1852 indicates that Josefa Pérez Soto, by then a widow, had moved to Monterey with her younger children, where the atmosphere towards the old *Californios* was far more hospitable.

*I knew they would never take me, but I was worried about my sons and my grandchildren. The night they came for the Hernandez boy, we could see the procession of torches leading up the hill to the jail. They took young Mariano and two others from their cells and left them hanging until noon of the next day. I tell you, **mi hijo**, the villa was never the same after that.*

Sometime in the late 1860s or early 1870s, Josefa returned to Santa Cruz, where she resided with her eldest son, Ramon Soto, on East Water Street. After her son's death on January 20, 1885, she was forced to move into a log cabin near the present site of Branciforte Elementary School. Her youngest daughter, Carmen Soto Leggett, lived down the street. It was then that the strong-willed Josefa began her morning journey for supplies along Pacific Avenue.

Less than four months after her son's death, on May 3, 1885, the following item appeared in the Santa Cruz *Sentinel*:

> Old Chapa [sic] was so drunk Wednesday that she fell
> and lay in the middle of Church Street until Officer
> Tainton procured an express wagon and hauled her home.
> When it is remembered that this woman is nearly a
> hundred years old, it is a crying shame for anyone to
> give or sell her liquor.

Could they wonder why I drank, mi hijo? To be so poor and laughed at in the town of my birth was a great pain, a very great pain, mi hijo. And to bury my son, Ramon—the death of one's child, ah, that is another great pain to bear. The spirit water put death to that pain, such a miserable pain.

During the following years, Josefa was in and out of the County Hospital. In 1889, she was there for three months.

They put me in the white man's house of medicine, and I will tell you, it was no place to be. I had been taught the spirit medicine of the Ohlone as a young girl, and I had used it all my life. If you want to know the truth, I think they wanted me out of the way. I was a bent up old woman, with the owl spirit in my heart, mi hijo, but the white man did not understand.

Scream? Of course, I screamed while I was in there. My dreams were frightening when I was there, the white walls and white linen. I will tell you, that was no place to die.

Josefa returned to her cabin and resumed her daily journeys downtown. Shortly thereafter, in the spring of 1890, she took ill again and was moved into the home of her daughter, Mrs. Leggett, on East Water Street. She died there—this woman

11

who had lived under four flags and who had outlived her times—on the morning of May 17, 1890. Her funeral was held at Holy Cross Church, the site of the old mission.

A short obituary in the Santa Cruz *Sentinel* referred to Josefa as "Mother Chapar" and declared: "Into her hands people have placed many ten-cent pieces, for she had a habit of asking for money. She could only speak a few words of English and observed to the last the quaint Mexican customs." A much longer and thorough obituary, undoubtedly written by the young reporter Ernest Otto, appeared in the Santa Cruz *Daily Surf* under the headline "Old Chepa: Death of a Local Character, Born with the Century."

"Although the year of her birth is surrounded by considerable obscurity, it seems certain, at least, that she was a contemporary of the present nineteenth century, and was not less than 90 years old, possibly several years more." She was buried in the old mission cemetery, just northeast of the Catholic Church.

*Come back to the hill of the mission again, **mi hijo**, and I will dance for you as I did when I was young. And I will tell you more stories, many more stories. What a long life, **mi hijo**. So many stories to tell.*

—1988

HANGING ON THE WATER STREET BRIDGE:
A Santa Cruz Lynching

BY THE TIME THE SUN rose on the morning of May 3, 1877, the two bodies dangling from the Water Street Bridge were already stiff from rigor mortis. A large crowd had gathered on the banks of the San Lorenzo River to gape at the hanging corpses, victims of an angry lynch mob the night before. It was well into mid-morning before the bodies were finally cut down. The remaining spectators, including children, called out bids for pieces of the death ropes, which had been sliced into foot-long sections for souvenirs.

"Judge Lynch had evidently been holding court," the Santa Cruz *Sentinel* observed, "but who the Judge, jury or attorneys were was purely a matter of conjecture."

The bodies of two men, Francisco Arias and José Chamales, were taken to a local undertaker's, where five Santa Cruzans were impaneled as an impromptu coroner's jury. Their verdict was predictable: "The deceased met their end on the upper San Lorenzo bridge at the hands of parties unknown." It's likely that at least one member of the jury had been a part of the lynch mob that hung the two men.

Arias and Chamales were of Mexican and Native American descent, and their's was not the first lynching of *Californios* by Santa Cruz's growing, often racist white population in the nineteenth century. As early as 1851, vigilantes hung Mariano Hernandez after pulling him out of the local jail, and there would be numerous other lynchings of *Californios* here in the ensuing quarter-century.

In certain respects, however, the lynching of Arias and Chamales marked the end of an era. Such incidents had become commonplace throughout California since the early days of the Gold Rush, but the Arias-Chamales hanging, at least temporarily, signaled a brief recess to anti-Mexican hostility. For most of the next decade, Chinese laborers became the primary targets of racist vigilante violence.

The immediate events that led to the Santa Cruz lynching began on the evening of Saturday, April 29, 1877, when Henry de Forrest, aged 62 and a carpenter at the local Powder Mill, was walking home along River Street near the site of the present Farmers Exchange. De Forrest, a native of Maine, was hoping to save up enough money to send for his wife and young children who remained on the east coast.

Near eight o'clock that evening, de Forrest was approached by two assailants and shot with a large caliber revolver through the chest. His pockets were ransacked, and he was dragged some 50 feet away from the main thoroughfare. It wasn't until the following morning that his body was found by a passerby.

An investigation of the murder was immediately organized by the county sheriff. According to local newspaper reports,

14

an unidentified *Californio* living in the Native American village a mile north of town had been stopped by two men, Arias and Chamales, just prior to the murder. The alleged assailants recognized their would-be victim and allowed him to proceed.

A short time later, the *Californio* declared, he heard a pistol discharged from where he had been accosted by Arias and Chamales.

Arias, a native of Pescadero, was 35 years old. He had served out two sentences at San Quentin, one for robbery, the other for murdering a sheep herder. Chamales, just 21 and a native of Santa Cruz, had also served time in San Quentin on a robbery conviction. The two men were seen together at the Aptos Circus following the time of the murder, and they were said to be in possession of substantial gold and silver coinage.

Other circumstantial evidence pointed towards Arias and Chamales as the murderers, including statements made by Chamales' mother. On Monday, Sheriff's deputies tracked down the two suspects, Chamales being found in Watsonville and Arias camped out with two women on the road to San Juan Bautista.

Both men, according to the papers, admitted to the murder, though Chamales supposedly fingered Arias as the actual assailant, claiming that it was Arias who pulled the trigger and that he himself had received only $2.50 of the $20 in coin taken from the victim. They were placed in the jail together on Tuesday.

It is at this point where accounts of the events diverge considerably. According to the three Santa Cruz papers—the *Sentinel, Local Item* and *Courier*—150 to 300 local residents descended on the jail during the night of Wednesday, May 2, and demanded the release of Arias and Chamales. From there the two prisoners were brought to the Water Street Bridge, where they were allowed a few last words (spoken in Spanish) and a final shot of whiskey. Then they were hanged.

Two other northern California papers, the *Bulletin* and the

Alta, disputed the figures which the local weeklies attributed to the lynch mob, both claiming that the number was closer to 40 or 50 men.

They also reported that the vigilantes wore masks or blackened faces to hide their identities, facts which the local papers omitted or denied, the implication being that the lynch mob did not have the vast community support which the local papers had claimed.

In either case, the non-Santa Cruz papers were sharply critical of the lynching. "Is the taking of human life without authority of law any less a murder because it is perpetrated by many instead of one?" asked the *Alta*. "Indeed not."

All three local papers, on the other hand, defended the lynching. According to the *Courier*, the lynch party "appeared to be officered . . . and showed a determination only born of mature deliberation," adding that "it would be economy to kill off a certain proportion of the criminal classes annually or else transport them."

Ironically, the *Courier* had taken the opposite view just two months earlier when there had been public sentiment aired towards lynching a white murder suspect. "Mobs are cowardly, cruel and unjust," the paper then declared, "and all who encourage or sustain this mode of correcting evils of society where the law can be enforced as it can be in Santa Cruz County, are unsafe exponents of public opinion."

—1984

CLIMBING GOLDEN MOUNTAIN

There are but a few Chinese in Santa Cruz,
because our people hate them, dread them,
despise them.

      —Duncan McPherson, 1882

IT IS THE SUMMER OF 1885 and three young children are peering into a barbershop on Front Street a few steps from where the Veterans' Memorial Building still stands today. If the children could be stirred to look up, they would see row upon row of rusty horseshoes nailed to the old wooden structure or the barber's sign, "Sing Lee and Front Street," tacked above the door. But their attention is not to be swayed from the scene taking place inside.

17

Sing Lee, the barber, is carefully unbraiding long strands of silk interwoven with the coarse, black hair of his customer. He disentangles the hair with a wooden comb, then applies near-boiling water to his customer's face and forescalp.

With a small triangular razor, he scrapes away the hair until the scalp is almost bleeding. In his left hand he is holding a wooden tray close to his customer's shoulder so that the hair does not fall to the floor. He shaves the ears and the skin between the eyes, places the razor on a stool and, finally, re-braids the silk and the hair from the back of the skull into a foot-long queue, or pigtail.

All of this surely fascinates the diminutive onlookers, but the barbershop provides an even more curious attraction than the shaving of a Chinaman: Sing Lee has six fingers on his right hand.

The children stare at the small piece of flesh and bone pro-truding from the barber's right thumb. One of them giggles, then another. Sing Lee turns and glares back at his young audience through the window of his shop.

What the children see in those brown eyes set in eternity is a matter of speculation. Perhaps they see the rice fields and ancient temples of the great land to the west from which Sing Lee ventured. Perhaps they see the torch lights which would come to drive Sing Lee and 300 of his fellow countrymen away from the city of the Holy Cross.

Or perhaps they see even further into the future—to the parking lots and concrete buildings which would come to serve as a mausoleum for a time that once was and would never be again.

The children look nervously at one another. It is getting near the noon hour and, without saying a word, they hurry back to their homes.

The Chinese community in which "Sing Lee and Front Street" conducted business a century ago was the second of four Santa Cruz Chinatowns. The first was located on what is now Pacific Avenue, between Walnut and Lincoln Streets, and dates as far back as 1859.

It lasted until the 1870s, when downtown business merchants shifted their center of activity from Front Street to Pacific Avenue and the Chinese moved to the quieter location on Front Street. In spite of considerable anti-Chinese sentiment and activity, that Chinatown lasted for nearly two decades, boasting a population of well over 100 residents, 10 laundries, three herb stores, opium dens and gambling halls.

Then in 1894 the Great Santa Cruz Fire, which destroyed the County Courthouse on Cooper Street and much of the downtown business district, also claimed the Front Street Chinatown as a victim. Many of the Santa Cruz Chinese, particularly members of the Gee Kong Tong (or Chinese Free Masons), moved to the Blackburn Ranch on West Sycamore Street near the Southern Pacific Railroad Depot.

Still other members of the Front Street community (many of whom belonged to the Congregational Association of Christian Chinese) moved around the corner to Bellevue Place, which ran east to the San Lorenzo River from where Cooper Street intersects with Front Street. The Chinese set up residence there in a series of ramshackle homes owned by a prosperous German immigrant, George Birkenseer.

There were numerous other Chinese communities in Santa Cruz County during the late 1800s: a small colony of Chinese who harvested abalone and seaweed just north of Davenport; another colony of about 30 fishermen just south of Capitola at what is now New Brighton State Beach; small camps of railroad workers throughout the San Lorenzo Valley; and a large Chinatown in Watsonville.

But Birkenseer's—located approximately where Coast Commercial Bank and the U.A. Theatres now stand—was the fourth and final Santa Cruz Chinatown. During the 1920s, white residents from as far away as San Jose and Fresno would flock into Birkenseer's to gamble, womanize, drink white whiskey, and a few, even, to smoke opium. Locals came to have their clothes washed or to purchase herbs. At least 14 buildings were occupied by the Chinese there as late as 1928.

"It was a lively place back then," remembered the late Malio Stagnaro, a Santa Cruz native who sold fish to the Chinese back in the Twenties. "Always lots of gambling, good food. The Chinese treated their patrons well."

By the mid-1930s, however, local authorities began cracking down on the gambling, drugs and bordellos (which were then owned and operated exclusively by whites in Birkenseer's), so that by the beginning of World War II, only four dwellings were occupied by the Chinese.

In 1952, all but one of the Chinatown shacks were boarded and vacant. Mrs. Gue She Lee, her second husband Arnold Sirna, and her youngest son, Jun Lee, were the last residents of Chinatown. When the flood of 1955 swept through the city, they, too, were forced to leave and make way for the redevelopment project which brought Albertson's, Longs and the UA Theaters to Santa Cruz.

The bulldozers did their dirty work and the last remnants of the Santa Cruz Chinatown crumbled. All that remained were the ghosts.

There are some who believe that the first Chinese to come to the Americas arrived here over a thousand years ago on sturdy wooden junks capable of trans-Pacific voyages. Anthropologists have noted striking similarities between symbols used by the Olemec tribes of Mexico and the peoples of Southern China, but so far positive proof of such cross-cultural interaction has yet to be established. In any event, the first confirmed Chinese immigrant to California was a cook named Ah Nam, who arrived in Monterey some time before 1815.

Mid-nineteenth century China, much like Ireland on the other side of the earth, was a nation plagued by war, floods, famine and banditry. The nation had recently been defeated by Great Britain in the Opium War of 1840, leaving the Chinese economy virtually in ruins.

Word that gold had been discovered in California quickly spread through Hong Kong to China's coastal provinces. Thousands of young men, almost all of them from the Canton region, journeyed across the Pacific, hoping to bring back enough wealth to alleviate the misery of their impoverished families.

By 1860, over 30,000 Chinese "pioneers," mostly between the ages of 17 and 35, migrated to the land of the "Golden Mountain."

While they were greeted with curiosity upon their arrival in San Francisco, the Chinese met with considerable hostility in the goldfields of the Sierra Nevada. They were often run off of their claims, scores were killed, and the promise of a fast fortune turned to dust.

Many of the Chinese driven from the mines took positions with the Central Pacific Railroad Company. "Without them," the Central's president, Leland Stanford declared, "it would be impossible to finish the western portion of this great national highway." It was largely with Chinese labor that the Central Pacific completed the monumental task of laying track over the rugged Sierras and across the Nevada and Utah deserts.

Still other unsuccessful miners filtered back to the coast. Many Chinese came to Santa Cruz County, and once here they also found railroad work. They dug tunnels and laid track from Los Gatos to Santa Cruz for the South Pacific Coast Railroad, and from Santa Cruz to Watsonville for F.A. Hihn's narrow-gauge rail.

At least 31 Chinese shovel workers were killed in 1878 while digging the mile-long Summit Tunnel in the Santa Cruz Mountains. When the railroads were finished, most Chinese found work as day laborers, domestic help or in laundries.

Reports published by the U.S. Census Bureau indicate that there were 156 Chinese living in Santa Cruz County in 1870, 523 in 1880, and a peak of 785 in 1890 when the county's white population totaled less than 20,000.

21

The most prominent feature of the Santa Cruz Chinatown was its absence of women. Reports vary, but it can be reasonably assumed that there were less than two dozen Chinese women living here at any one time prior to 1920. Santa Cruz was not unique in this aspect. In 1890, for instance, the ratio of Chinese men to women in California was 22 to 1.

Chinese custom of the nineteenth century dictated that wives were to remain in the home, even when their husbands went abroad. Many Chinese women during this period still had their feet bound. Those women who came to California were largely unmarried, widowed, or the wives of wealthy merchants.

The Chinese Exclusion Act of 1882, which restricted the immigration of Chinese laborers, also barred the entrance of their wives. After 1882 those Chinese men who were already working in California could not call on their families to join them.

Thus the Chinatowns of the West Coast were "bachelor societies"—societies in which the men were lonely and sexually frustrated, while the women were outcasts and often abused. The few Chinese women immigrants who weren't married to merchants frequently found themselves serving as unwilling prostitutes. Many were brought here exclusively for that purpose.

Although it does not state so specifically, the U.S. Commerce report for Santa Cruz County in 1880 hints at the existence of seven Chinese prostitutes in the Front Street Chinatown. The report identifies seven "unemployed women" living with a male "cook" at a single residence. The women were unrelated. That this could have been anything but a bordello is unlikely.

Given the absence of any family structure, California Chinatowns were organized on large-scale social units. One such level of organization was the secret society or "tong." These societies developed in China during the seventeenth century to oppose the Manchu dynasty, and they reproduced themselves on the West Coast.

In Santa Cruz, virtually all of the Chinese prior to 1890 were members of the Gee Kong Tong, or Chinese Free Masons. They met in a temple called a "joss house" by whites, where they unbraided their queues (marks of subjection mandated by the Manchus) and repeated oaths to free their native land.

There were temples at each of the four Chinatowns, the last being located on the banks of the San Lorenzo River near the present-day UA Theatres. It was torn down in 1950.

"The interior of the joss house," according to Ernest Otto, "featured pictures of ancient heroes of China who had become deified. The shrine was in an alcove at one end of the room. A continuing burning light was before the shrine.

"Smoke from burning incense of sandalwood, punks and red candles had, through the years, so blackened the figures on the sacred pictures, the characters could scarcely be seen."

The leader of the Santa Cruz secret society was Wong Kee, a colorful local merchant who on holidays, Otto recalled, "wore a black horsehair skull cap topped with buttons of red silk or coral beads" and robes which were "in tones of emerald green, Chinese reds, lavender, and navy blue." The local whites referred to him as "the town mayor."

Wong Kee's store was located in the only brick building in Chinatown. In it could be found copper pots, kettles, ribbon, firecrackers, rice, oysters, shark fins, sweet bamboo sprouts, okra, teas, hams and dried fish.

The second floor housed a gambling hall, where "fan tan," "pie gow," and Chinese checkers were played. All business transactions were calculated on an abacus.

Another joss house was located at the California Powder Works on the San Lorenzo River, where Paradise Park is presently located. Scores of Chinese men (perhaps as many as 100) lived and worked there during the 1870s, when the company had one of the two government contracts to produce smokeless gun powder for the U.S. Army.

The other major organization in Chinatown was the Congregational Association of Christian Chinese. It was founded here in 1881 by the Reverend Mahlon Willet. Later, a Chinese cook and merchant named Pon Fang was sent to Santa Cruz by Willet's missionary group to head the Chinese congregation.

In 1892 Pon Fang established the first "Chinese Christian Endeavor Society" in the United States. Forty residents of the Santa Cruz Chinatown were members. The society met on Friday nights, Pon Fang teaching his followers how to read and write English along with the fundamentals of Christianity.

Since he was a merchant, Pon Fang was able to bring his wife and young son, Samuel, to the U.S. His wife (whose name apparently was never recorded in the press) was the first woman in the Santa Cruz Chinatown to have bound feet. While living here she gave birth to four more children: Joseph, Ruth, Esther and Daniel.

After the Great Earthquake and Fire of 1906, the population of the Santa Cruz Chinatown began to dwindle and interest waned in the Congregational mission. Pon Fang, like many local Chinese, moved to San Francisco, taking his family with him.

Aside from performing tasks as day laborers, many Chinese men worked in the laundry business. In 1880 there were already 19 Chinese laundries in the county, employing 70 workers full time. Ten were located in downtown Santa Cruz.

Because most white males felt laundry work beneath their dignity, the Chinese were able to enter the wash house business with a minimum of resistance. Chinese laundries were labor intensive and required little initial investment. They rapidly became the foundation of the Chinese economy.

On entering a Chinese laundry, Otto recalled in one of his historical columns, "One saw a long ironing board against the wall on each side, with six or seven men ironing . . . At the side of each was a sauce bowl filled with water set on top of a starch box. The Chinese, wearing white cotton blouses, would bend over to fill their mouths with water and then spray it over the clothes to dampen them." Rocks behind the wash houses were used for beating the clothes.

Chinese gardeners provided the Santa Cruz community with a large supply of its fresh fruits and vegetables. In 1885 the Santa Cruz *Surf* reported 125 "soil cultivators" in the city earning $20 a month. One large Chinese garden was located at the Blackburn Ranch near Chestnut and West Sycamore Streets, and another off King Street above what is now Mission Hill Junior High.

Henry Biekiewicz, a Polish visitor to the West Coast in the 1870s, reported that "the fruits and vegetables, raspberries, and strawberries under the care of Chinese gardeners grow to a fabulous size. I have seen strawberries as large as small pears and heads of cabbage four times the size of European heads." Chinese vegetable peddlers sold their produce from overflowing baskets balanced on shoulder poles.

The first commercial fishing in Monterey Bay was done by the Chinese, although that industry, particularly after 1880, was centered on the Monterey Peninsula. The Santa Cruz Chinese—like their counterparts in San Francisco and New York—developed close ties with the Italian fishing colony. The Italians provided Chinatown with a variety of fish (petrale sole, gopher cod, octopus and pompano), which the Chinese dried on racks located near the San Lorenzo River.

When the Chinese weren't working (and perhaps even when they were), they were often under the influence of opium. The British had imported the habit from India to China in the nineteenth century, and the Chinese brought it with them to America.

Otto claimed that the drug was smoked by a "high percentage" of the local Chinese population. Nearly every shop or laundry had a small room or den set aside for opium consumption. The room usually had a selection of water pipes and a mattress of some sort on which the user could pass out.

One of the biggest opium busts in the history of Santa Cruz

Chinatown took place on November 25, 1925. Wong Tai Yut was arrested that day by the local sheriff with "two large tins" of the drug estimated in value at $400.

By far the greatest celebration in Chinatown occurred during the Chinese New Year. The Chinese stopped working for three days and prepared huge, elaborate meals for the festivities. "Dinners were served with the finest delicacies," Otto recalled, "pork, chicken, bird's nest soup and shark fins."

On February 1, 1915 the local daily reported that "the Chinese New Year was ushered in last night by a fusillade of firecrackers, feasting and worship. But the New Year is observed less and less each year as the Chinatown population decreases..."

By then, wounds from an ugly chapter in Santa Cruz history may have been forgotten—but they had surely taken their toll.

To state that the Chinese were "driven out" of Santa Cruz, as some historians have suggested, is to oversimplify greatly the complex web of social, political and economic forces which eventually resulted in the demise of the local Chinese community; but certainly, the whites did attempt to drive them out.

There were three great waves of anti-Chinese sentiment here, the first beginning in the late 1870s, the second in 1882 and the third commencing in 1885. At the center of all three was Duncan McPherson, editor and publisher of the Santa Cruz *Sentinel.*

In 1879 a *Sentinel* editorial written by McPherson characterized the Chinese as "half-human, half-devil, rat-eating, rag-wearing, law-ignoring, Christian civilization-hating, opium smoking, labor-degrading, entrail-sucking Celestials."

McPherson, of course, was not the only racist in the state, and California's anti-Chinese movement did not begin here in Santa Cruz. As early as 1850 the Chinese were referred to in the press as "rats," "mongrels" and "low-animals." In the winter of 1867, the first formal anti-Coolie organization drove laborers away from their jobs on San Francisco's Potrero Hill. A few months later, a Chinese vegetable peddler was stoned to death there by an angry mob of youths.

The incipient anti-Chinese sentiment spread throughout the West Coast and culminated in 1877 with the establishment of the Workingmen's Party of California. While its platform contained a number of decidedly radical proposals designed to redistribute wealth, the Workingmen's Party was first and foremost an anti-Chinese organization. Its demagogic leader, Denis Kearney, called for the immediate deportation of all Chinese laborers from the state.

"Are you ready to march down to the wharf and stop the leprous Chinaman from landing?" Kearney once addressed an angry mob. "The dignity of labor must be sustained even if we have to kill every wretch that opposes it. . . The Chinese must go!"

By January of 1878 the Workingmen's Party had become a major political force in California.

Seventy-five miles down the coast, the Workingmen's organization took on a uniquely Santa Cruz flavor. In San Francisco the organization was made up largely of white workers— men and women who feared their livelihoods were threatened by cheap Chinese labor. In Santa Cruz, where the Chinese generally didn't compete with whites for jobs, the Workingmen were composed largely of the landed gentry and businessmen.

The president of the local Workingmen's club was Elihu Anthony, a wealthy industrialist, landowner and Methodist minister. Its most vociferous sympathizer was McPherson, who not only published the *Sentinel,* but according to E.H. Harrison's *History of Santa Cruz,* had "more buildings in this city than any other man."

Suspiciously missing from the Santa Cruz Workingmen's platform were the party's plans for redistributing wealth, save for occasional attacks on the railroads. An entire section of the platform, however, was devoted exclusively to the Chinese:

"Chinese cheap labor is a curse to our land, a menace to our liberties and the institutions of our country and should be restricted and forever abolished; and no citizen shall be eligible for membership into this club who employs or knowingly patronizes in any form, shape or manner that class of people known as the Chinese."

The first direct action taken by the local Workingmen was aimed at the Chinese laundries. In March 1880 the club requested that the Santa Cruz City Council remove all Chinese wash houses from within the city limits. The Council balked at that blatantly racist proposal, but three months later passed a law which had a similar effect.

On June 5, 1880 the Council adopted the following ordinance: "No person shall carry baskets or bags attached to poles carried upon back or shoulders on public sidewalks." Chinese deliverers were forced from the safety of the sidewalks into the roadway, but the industry survived the restrictive legislation. The ordinance was later declared unconstitutional.

Meanwhile, the United States Congress in Washington was beginning to express concern with the growing anti-Chinese activities, sending a commission to the West Coast with orders to investigate the situation. In 1882 legislation was introduced in the Senate which would restrict Chinese immigration for 20 years.

Both houses of Congress passed the bill, but President Chester Arthur vetoed it on April 4 of the same year.

Santa Cruzans were irate with the President's decision. Three years earlier, County residents had voted 2540 to 4 in favor of restricting Chinese immigration, and they were determined to keep further Chinese from entering their community.

Arthur's veto spurred a spontaneous parade in downtown Santa Cruz. Fanned by the rhetoric of McPherson, who declared, "The Chinese are a scab on the face of our state," local residents burned Arthur's effigy at the lower downtown plaza.

Later that year, Arthur signed a slightly modified version of the Chinese Exclusion Act, which was amended in 1884, extended indefinitely in 1902, and wasn't repealed until 1943. For over 50 years, Chinese laborers and their wives were barred from entering this country.

The final great wave of the local anti-Chinese movement had its beginnings in February 1885 and culminated a year later. By then local Sino-racism was stripped of its Workingmen's facade. The state "Non-Partisan Anti-Chinese Association" had active clubs in Watsonville, Aptos, Boulder Creek and Felton. In downtown Santa Cruz, Anthony and McPherson remained at the forefront of the movement.

Once again Chinese laundries provided the initial focus for their attack. A health ordinance regulating sewage disposal was aimed directly at Chinese wash houses. Soon after the local association called for a boycott of all Chinese merchants (including vegetable peddlers) and even white-owned businesses which employed Chinese.

McPherson and his associates didn't stop there. Perhaps motivated by economic self-interest, the *Sentinel* publisher called for an extension of the boycott to include his competition, the Santa Cruz *Surf*, whose fiery editor, A.A. Taylor, had opposed the original boycott on the grounds that it divided the white community.

A vitriolic debate ensued between the two men. Finally, on December 14, 1885, Taylor played his trump card. "The poor man who buys a beet from a Chinaman's basket ought to be boycotted," the *Surf* editorial argued, "[but] the man who sells or rents to a Chinaman is a reformer and ought to be made governor."

In one of the great ironies of local history, it turned out that McPherson himself was the landlord of a Chinese laundry and that he had been collecting rent from the "entrail-sucking Celestials" for quite some time. "I have made a living out of the paper," McPherson once boasted, "and money out of real estate."

Taylor eventually won a lawsuit from the *Sentinel* and the paper's business manager was later cited by the state Anti-Coolie League "for failure to act in good faith."

The *Sentinel-Surf* battle, however, did little to curb local Sinophobia. On February 27 of the following year, the Anti-Chinese Association staged a county-wide torchlight parade down Pacific Avenue. Hundreds of association members participated in the march, carrying banners and shouting, "The Chinese must go!"

But the Chinese stayed. In what is surely a tribute to the internal solidity of their Front Street community, the Santa Cruz Chinese withstood the decade-long effort to drive them out. A major fire in 1887 and the Great Fire of 1894 finally forced them to move their community, but they did so largely on their own terms—and they didn't move far.

It would be all too easy to attribute the anti-Chinese sentiment which infested this area to the economic depression which struck California in the late 1870s and lasted for most of the following decade. Unemployment rates in San Francisco, for instance, skyrocketed during this period, a factor which certainly contributed to the bitterness of the white working class.

Such was not the case in Santa Cruz. There was some unemployment here, to be sure, but the whites were not competing with the Chinese for work. Rather, it seems more likely that the white business community feared the competition of successful Chinese merchants and attempted to drive them from the marketplace. Old-fashioned racism served as the axle of their movement, and the well-publicized bigotry of Duncan McPherson and his ilk greased it for over a decade.

While the boycotts and torchlight parades failed in their short-term objectives, they had long-term implications which eventually resulted in the demise of the Santa Cruz community. The restrictive legislation which outlawed the immigration of Chinese laborers and women cut the lifeline of the local

Chinatown. Business regulations prevented the Chinese from entering the economic mainstream. Without new blood or the opportunity for social mobility, the Chinese community atrophied. Only a handful of Chinatowns on the West Coast survived the subsequent economic and social decay.

In the 1980s, the Evergreen Cemetery which overlooks Harvey West Park is a quiet, serene setting, save for a few hikers and stray dogs who wander through its pathways. High up one of its southeastern slopes there is a sprawling bay tree and a cubic structure which looks something like a small incinerator.

Beneath the shadow of the sprawling bay are headstones with Chinese characters on them, another which reads "Chinese Burial Ground, January 1, 1901," and still another reading "Lee Song, 1851-1929." It was on this small plot of soil that most of the Santa Cruz Chinese were buried.

"Chinese funerals were elaborate affairs," according to Renie Leaman, a longtime friend of the cemetery. "Most of Chinatown turned out for the gatherings." When a member of the Santa Cruz community passed away, a seer or astrologer was consulted to discern the proper day to conduct the burial. Sometimes the wait lasted as long as two weeks.

A pair of horse-drawn wagons led the funeral processions, one carrying the casket, the other carrying wooden baskets loaded with oranges, apples, chickens, roast pig, firecrackers and all the possessions of the deceased.

Behind the carriages, men swirled paper streamers to scare away the devil. There were thousands of holes in the streamers, and the Chinese believed that the devil had to pass through each one in order to get to the dead person's soul. Occasionally, a member of the procession stomped on the streamer, hoping that the devil had become entangled in the holes. Firecrackers were also exploded to ward off evil spirits.

At the graveyard the casket and baskets were hauled up the hill. Chinese music and the smell of burning herbs filled the air. The deceased's possessions were set on fire in the holy oven, while the baskets of food were situated around the grave and some coins were placed in a plate so that the deceased would not go into the next life without wealth. But their bodies did not remain in Evergreen.

Many of the Chinese who came to Santa Cruz in the 1800s did not intend to stay here. Certainly, they did not intend to die here. After a body had been entombed for a decade, it was dug up by family members or friends, packaged, and sent back to China.

"This is a cherished burial custom," the *Sentinel* noted in an article dated November 4, 1925. "The Chinese believe that their bones should have as a final resting place the soil of their flowery kingdom, and no matter where they die, the bones are unearthed and sent to the burial ground of the villages of their birth." Eighteen bodies had been disinterred earlier that afternoon.

Scorned and oppressed in America, the Santa Cruz Chinese made sure that their spirits would not meet the same fate. The land of the Golden Mountain may have taken their sweat and blood, may have turned their dreams into dust and their culture into a laughing stock, but it would never claim their souls.

—1983

"THE SHAME OF CALIFORNIA"

*Among the multitudes in Santa Cruz this week,
there is no one man as eagerly inquired after,
so much sought out, as Abraham Ruef of San
Francisco...Without him, no Governor can
be named.*
　　　　　　　　—The Santa Cruz *Surf*
　　　　　　　　4 September 1906

SANTA CRUZ WAS BIG TIME once. In September of 1906, a
little less than five months following the great San Francisco
earthquake and fire, Santa Cruz played host to the Republican

State Convention, a thoroughly scandalous affair which was destined to be known as "the Shame of California." During a week of gala festivities, the Republicans sold their gubernatorial nominee in classic back-room fashion for $14,000 and political pocket change.

Hosted by the Seaside Company at its Canvas Casino along the main beach, the Santa Cruz convention proved to be the final hurrah for two of the West Coast's more prominent public figures: Abraham Ruef, San Francisco's wily political boss, and Major Frank McLaughlin of Santa Cruz—dilettante, reputed gunslinger, financier and chairman of the state Republican Central Committee. While the convention marked the zenith of the two men's political power, in little more than a year both of their careers would end suddenly in disgrace.

Swelled with tourists enjoying the final weeks of the summer season, Santa Cruz welcomed the Republicans with an assortment of parades and festivities. Arriving in Santa Cruz by rail, delegates to the convention were promptly escorted by marching bands along Pacific Avenue, which was elaborately decorated with redwood trees, colored lights, garlands of evergreen and 2,000 Japanese lanterns.

A crowd of 25,000 was expected for the convention's grand finale, a dawn-to-dusk Admissions Day celebration sponsored by the local chapter of the California Native Sons.

As the convention opened for business on September 5, the Republican nomination for governor was still very much in doubt—or more accurately, very much up for sale. Proclamations of an open convention to the contrary, the final decision was not to be made on the convention floor, but in Major McLaughlin's spacious Golden Gate Villa, the 20-room Third Street mansion which overlooks the Santa Cruz waterfront.

Then-incumbent Republican Governor George C. Pardee was something of an early-day progressive, and during his first term in office had initiated a series of anti-trust policies aimed directly at the state's railroads. In so doing, he earned the wrath of William F. Herrin, chief legal counsel and power broker of the Southern Pacific.

Since the late 1860s the railroad company had all but controlled California politics, buying and selling politicians as though they were tracts of land. In 1906, Herrin and the railroad wanted Pardee out; their man was James Gillett of Eureka.

Though Pardee and Gillett both claimed scattered statewide support, neither of them came to Santa Cruz with enough votes to secure the nomination. Only one man controlled enough delegate votes to swing the convention either way: Boss Ruef of San Francisco.

Southern Pacific's Herrin had only one option. Fully aware that Ruef held the destiny of the convention in his 159-member delegation, Herrin was forced to deal with the so-called "debonair boss" for his support of the Southern Pacific slate.

On the evening before the votes were to be cast, Ruef and Herrin met in McLaughlin's mansion and an agreement was finalized. Ruef would be allowed to name three state appellate judges and a slew of other state officials in exchange for the San Francisco delegation's support of the Southern Pacific candidate, Gillett. As an additional gesture of gratitude, Herrin delivered $14,000 in cash to Ruef for "delegate expenses" and then quickly got out of town.

Word that Ruef and Southern Pacific had struck a deal immediately spread through the convention. Pardee supporters were bitterly aware their candidate had been sold out in a classic back-room political bargain.

The Santa Cruz and Monterey delegations also got into the act, casting their votes for the railroad's candidate in exchange for the promise that Warren R. Porter of Watsonville would be nominated for Lieutenant Governor.

"The jig is up," the Santa Cruz *Surf* reported following Gillett's nomination. "The 'Organization' is in complete control of the Republican Party. Terms were made with Ruef last night, and this morning the machine moved without slipping a cog."

Following the convention's final gavel, Major McLaughlin hosted a lavish dinner party at his home. All of the significant players in the deal were present (with the exception of Herrin, who took the first train out of town) and it occurred to the Major that a photograph should be taken to preserve the moment for posterity.

The celebrators posed proudly for a group portrait. The diminutive Ruef was seated center-stage beside his buoyant host. Immediately behind him stood the nominee Gillett, his hand resting respectfully on the shoulder of the man who had just sold him his candidacy. The trio was flanked by an assortment of other candidates who owed their nominations to Ruef's patronage. Little did they know that their impromptu portrait was destined for infamy.

At least one of Ruef's corporals was apparently elated enough to write home about it. In a postcard addressed to a "Miss Gibson" in San Francisco (and which was later discovered by noted biologist Joel Hedgpeth of Santa Rosa), Congressman C.B. McLachlan, a minor foot soldier in the whole affair, boasted that he had "just secured the nomination of the next Governor of California."

Gillett and the Southern Pacific slate easily captured the statewide elections in November, but in San Francisco, Boss Ruef's fortunes were heading swiftly toward disaster.

For nearly a decade Ruef had run the city's government as though it were his private business, and had acquired great personal wealth in return for political favors, municipal construction contracts following the earthquake, and business licenses.

Appalled by the open corruption of the San Francisco machine, President Theodore Roosevelt assigned federal detectives to investigate Ruef and his associates. Less than two weeks following Gillett's election as governor, Ruef was indicted on extortion charges. Later convicted, he served four years and 10 months in San Quentin. The San Francisco machine was destroyed.

In an effort to discredit Gillett and the Southern Pacific slate, reform groups began posting copies of the convention photo on billboards across the state. Emblazoned in bold letters above the convicted Ruef and company read: "The Shame of California."

Here in Santa Cruz, however, Ruef's fate and the notorious photograph were the least of Major McLaughlin's concerns. A once-prosperous man who claimed the friendship of Thomas Edison and the prize fighter John L. Sullivan, McLaughlin participated in one shady mining venture too many, and by the autumn of 1907, his finances and spirits had reached rock bottom.

On November 16, the second anniversary of his wife's death, the troubled McLaughlin shot his daughter Agnes as she napped in the parlor of Golden Gate Villa. He then returned to his own room, where he swallowed a cupful of cyanide.

McLaughlin sent out at least 15 suicide notes, one of which was sent to the Santa Cruz *Sentinel.* "Please treat my memory as kindly as you can," it requested. The *Sentinel* obliged, referring to McLaughlin as a "man of princely instincts" and as "one of the bravest men ever residing on the West Coast."

At least one other newspaper, the Sacramento *Bee,* took a different view of the late Republican kingpin: "Show and Sham were Major McLaughlin's gods. He lived in their idolatry, and when he could no longer buy their favors, he put an end to his life, as though all that were really worth living for had departed forever...This deed, with its devilish preaching of the bastard duty of a father, should be reproved from one end of the state to another."

At the Major's request, the bodies were shipped to his native New York for burial.

—1982

A HISTORIAN FOR ALL TIME:
Santa Cruz Through the Eyes of Ernest Otto

"SOME THINGS WHICH A SMALL boy sees he never forgets..." Thus begins one of the many historical reminiscences which Ernest Otto wrote over the years for the Santa Cruz *Sentinel,* and a fortunate fact it is for those of us who have followed in his footsteps. Were it not for the memory of this single man, a good deal of Santa Cruz history would have been buried in the past forever.

Otto's sense of the historical had little to do with time and dates of particular events; rather, it focused on the actual feel and texture of periods in our past—periods which he brought back to life with his keen sensitivity to small details and everyday occurrences. In writing about a flood that took place in the 1880s, for instance, he described huge logs rushing down the "swirling waters of the San Lorenzo," floating "slowly to the mouth of the river, then shooting out into the breakers." And then with a touch that is purely Otto, he added that "most of the logs landed on the Seabright and Twin Lakes beaches where it was reclaimed for firewood."

Otto was a newspaper reporter in Santa Cruz for over 70 years. He began his journalism career in his early teens as a copy boy with the long-defunct *Courier-Item*, and from the beginning, he developed a reporting style that was uniquely his own. He was a "beat" reporter in the purest sense of the term, and no happening, great or small, ever seemed to escape his attention. As an "editor's note" in the 83rd Anniversary Edition of the *Sentinel* declared, "This paper will continue to be a healthy, newsy small town daily so long as Ernest Otto, dean of Santa Cruz papermen, considers it important to mention that Mrs. Jones' lettuce garden was destroyed by rabbits."

And that is why, over 30 years after his death, Otto is so important to us today. The stories that he filed daily, along with his "News from the Waterfront" and "Old Santa Cruz" columns, provide us with a window to our past that would have otherwise been boarded shut long ago. Through the writings of Otto, we can watch as young children in the 1880s scamper up Mission Hill to watch a hanging at the old city jail. We can smell the herbs and opium emanating from the shops in Chinatown or the fresh catches of salmon and mackerel on the municipal pier. We can hear the sounds of the Suntan Special lumbering through the Santa Cruz Mountains or the German cobbler peddling his wares on Pacific Avenue. We can taste the minestrone soup in the homes of the old Italian women in the Westside barranca or the straight shots of whiskey in an old Irish saloon. And we can know the pain in the heart of "Mrs. Jones" when she found her lettuce eaten by the rabbits. No, indeed, nothing was too small to escape the note pad of Ernest Otto.

The man who would one day come to be known as "Mr. Santa Cruz" was born in a wood-framed home near the corner of Church and Cedar Streets in 1871, less than 20 yards, ironically, from the site of the present *Sentinel* offices. His parents were both of German stock and natives of Baltimore. His father, George Otto, first immigrated to Santa Cruz in 1851, and Otto's mother, Gertrude, followed some 12 years later. There were eight children in the Otto clan, and from all accounts, it was a happy, though well-disciplined household.

Ernest attended Mission Hill Grammar and Junior High School, and while there developed a fascination for newspapers that never was to leave him. At the age of ten, in 1881, he began delivering the *Courier-Item,* and later delivered the Santa Cruz *Surf, Daily Sentinel, Daily Echo,* and also out-of-town papers, including the *Chronicle* and *Examiner.* Soon he began carrying copy and proof at the *Courier-Item,* where he also contributed "notes" from around town he had gathered on deliveries. By the time he was 18, he was a full-time reporter with the Santa Cruz *Surf,* published and edited by Arthur Taylor. In his own words, he was "the lone reporter on a one-reporter paper."

In a column written in 1947, Otto described his daily routine as a fledgling cub reporter with the *Surf.* With only minor variation, it was a routine which he was to stick to all the rest of his life.

Otto would leave his home at 11 a.m. and make his way down to the Southern Pacific train station on Washington Street, where he "tried to keep tab of those leaving on the train of five or six coaches. Keeping track of these travelers meant many personal items for the paper, and in addition, the contacts would give reports on the goings and comings of other people." Santa Cruz, even back then, was a tourist town, and tourism was a central element of Otto's beat. After leaving the station, he would continue by foot (he never drove his entire life) to the various hotels in the city, checking their registers "for notables who might be visiting the city."

Later in the day, he would meet the incoming train, where

he would pick up the latest edition of the San Francisco papers. From there he would make his way to his various governmental sources—the county courthouse, city hall, the justice of the peace, the fire department, the police station, the board of supervisors, and, finally, the undertaker.

This last stop carried a personal Otto touch. Never content to write merely the bare essentials of the deceased, Otto always contacted their families and friends, compiling intimate details about them which gave meaning to their lives. Although obituaries were never by-lined, of course, there is no mistaking those that were written by Otto. Who else would choose to note that Mrs. Beatrice Johnson kept a turnip garden or that Robert Taylor enjoyed catching reptiles as a child? Many of the deceased had been personal friends of his, and he wanted their final remembrance to do justice to their lives. Later in his career he proudly acknowledged that his obituaries "were seldom less than half a column long."

It was "in between" his official sources, however, that Otto captured the heartbeat of the city. Until the time of his death, his daily trek was no less than six miles, and he came to know just about everyone who lived here. If something was happening in the neighborhoods of Santa Cruz, Otto knew about it— from the rabbits in Mrs. Jones' garden to whether or not the Tara boys were cutting school. And it all—or at least most of it—found its way into the paper.

An essential part of Otto's routine in the late nineteenth century was a stroll through the Front Street Chinatown, and following its destruction by fire, the Birkenseer Chinatown across from Cooper Street. Otto felt entirely at home there, where he "knew every merchant and spoke to most of the 300 inhabitants, calling them by name."

Near the turn of the century, Otto added another venue to his daily stroll, the old railroad wharf and its burgeoning Genovese-Italian fishing colony. In 1919, when he was hired as the city editor of the Santa Cruz *Sentinel,* Otto began publishing daily notes from his strolls along the new municipal pier, notes which soon turned into his famous "Waterfront" column. You can go back to almost any week in Santa Cruz waterfront history and look up in amazing detail exactly what was going on along the wharf. During the week of May 12, 1937, for instance, Otto noted the amount of rock fish caught by seven different commercial fishermen, the salmon catches on the Stagnaro party boats, and the various games being played by visitors on the main beach.

Otto also wrote regularly about the city's various religious communities, and this may well have been the issue closest to his heart. On January 3, 1893, he joined the First Congregational Church, of which he served as clerk for 57 years. Near his 70th birthday, the church held a special day in his honor and paid tribute to him with a proclamation which declared in part: "Ernest Otto stands as a splendid example of volunteer workers who make the Christian church the great institution it is. Of his faithfulness there shall be no end. His life and work in Santa Cruz is living proof of the value of service and good life." Lillian McPherson Rouse, who knew Otto for many years and was a fellow church member, recalls that it was rare indeed for Otto to ever miss a Sunday service.

Given his rather grand public persona, Otto's personal life seems somewhat cramped. While he had many friends, he never married and lived alone for over 40 years. He was a tee-totaler his entire life, having had a horrifying experience with wine at the age of ten. He was not, however, a blue-nose, and according to an account in the *Sentinel,* he once came to the defense of a man who had been berated for his drinking. "Some people," he declared, "are better drunk than others are sober." For exercise, he swam daily in the ocean, often accompanied by his friends.

Otto enjoyed the theater and the opera, and occasionally journeyed to San Francisco by train to take in performances there. His longest journey away from Santa Cruz was in 1950, when at the age of 79, he took a six-week vacation along the eastern seaboard. Always dressed in a hat, suit and tie, he was short in stature, had round, boyish features, and by most accounts, always had a warm, ingratiating smile. During his youth he sported a moustache. Robert Stagnaro of the municipal pier has possession of a tape recording of Otto, made during a waterfront celebration in 1943, and Otto's voice was strong, if a little gravelly.

Otto apparently wrote very quickly, and his typewritten copy contained a fair share of errors. Mrs. Rouse possesses a short three-page story of what must be the last original Otto copy in existence; on it, Otto made over 30 handwritten corrections, using many of the old newspaper signs that have long been out of use.

Of the dozen or so former friends and acquaintances interviewed for this portrait, no one had even the slightest thing bad to say about the man, but there were also very few details about his personal life that they could recall. Most described him as "nice" and "sincere," "friendly" and "intelligent," and that he always had a notebook in hand. Gilda Stagnaro declared that "Mr. Otto was the most dignified man I ever met," while Lillian McPherson Rouse recalls "the twinkle in his eyes." Beyond that, little else seems to have been known. He kept his private life exceedingly private. He was always with the people, but never entirely of them. To the Santa Cruz community he was thus something of an enigma, albeit a familiar enigma, and a much beloved and highly-respected one at that.

Margaret Koch notes in her *Santa Cruz County: Parade of the Past* that Otto always received a flood of gifts at the paper during the holidays:

> One Christmas he received (by actual count at the newspaper) 40 jars of fruit, six boxes of candy, 10 fruit cakes, a smoking jacket from "a Chinese friend"; a wallet from another "Chinese friend"; $10 in cash mailed from Italy, a shoeshine from "a colored friend," delicacies from the Municipal Wharf, several hundred greeting cards, and other small articles too numerous to list.

To get at the essence of Ernest Otto, however, we must return to his writings—and sometimes we must read between the lines. While we can catch glimmers of the man in some of his un-bylined earlier work, it is in his later "Old Santa Cruz" columns that the true Otto persona emerges. Otto began writing the historical columns formally in 1939. Then *Sentinel* editor Fred McPherson, Jr., immediately recognized the historic value of the pieces, suggesting to *Sentinel* readers in an editor's note that they should "clip these articles for later reference."

As has been noted, Otto wrote about anything and everything, but it is possible, nonetheless, to categorize his writing into a handful of useful subheadings. A small, though significant portion of Otto's historical columns cover the natural history of Santa Cruz, both its geography and wildlife. He seems to have been familiar with every gulch and creek in the county, and he knew them as if they were in his own back yard. Other columns recount the wildlife that used to inhabit Santa Cruz County, including mountain lions, badgers and grizzly bears:

> One story the Otto children often heard their father repeat was of being attacked by a bear while returning by horseback from San Francisco. In the mountains near Pescadero the bear, with its claws, tore the flesh off the back of the horse and the coat of the rider. He set up a yell which frightened the bear. The father looked back and could see the bear standing up, watching the horse and rider.

Otto also paid keen attention to Santa Cruz architecture, noting when a certain home or church was built, and both who designed and constructed it. Taken together, Otto's pieces on the natural history and architecture of Santa Cruz provide us with a three-dimensional relief map of the community a century ago.

Another category of Otto's writings involve special get-togethers, festivals and social gatherings. He seems to have been captivated as a boy by such festivities, no doubt in part because they lightened the load of his life of school, church and endless family chores. He loved to sneak his way into the theater and into ballrooms, where he could watch couples dancing late into the night—and sometimes into the streets.

> It was not uncommon to see Florence Vasquez and Devee Thompson stroll along the streets toward evening, with, slung over their shoulders, their guitars, favorite musical instrument of the Spanish. At the cascarone dances, egg shells filled with bits of colored paper were broken over the men's heads by the ladies.

Otto was also struck by the many "characters" who inhabited Santa Cruz and who, no doubt, contrasted strikingly with the plain, straightforward nature of his German parents. He wrote about professional gamblers and gunslingers, drunks and assorted ne'er-do-wells. One of his favorites was "Old Billy Duffey," who lived out near Soquel.

> ...He rode in his deep blue dumpcart and would greet his friends with the richest brogue. He never missed coming to town on St. Patrick's Day with a bow of green ribbons. The writer well remembers when he moved to town he was passing the Duffey house on Laurel Street, when suddenly there was a shaking from an earthquake and Billy came out at great speed from the house with a newspaper in his hand, followed by his wife, who was somewhat crippled, crying, "Oh Billy, Billy, Billy." His reply was, "Aw, everyone for himself at the time of an earthquake."

Like most products of Nineteenth Century America, Otto viewed the New World's human community in terms of its ethnic composition, but unlike most of his contemporaries, he seems not to have been weighted by racism or prejudice. Certainly, his deeply held religious beliefs contributed to his equanimity, but that can only serve as a partial explanation, as many with similar religious backgrounds were often some of the county's worst bigots. Otto's inherent love of humanity simply knew no bounds, and he wrote about people of all colors, races and creeds with equal sensitivity and respect.

Otto's childhood corresponded with the era that marked the last days of native Ohlones and mixed-blooded *Californios* in Santa Cruz. Among the subjects for his columns was "Old Roxas," the elderly Ohlone who reportedly lived to 114 and who was well known throughout the city. "He always had his cane," Otto remembered, "and for years wore the same browned and tattered straw hat. Born here, baptized in the old Mission, he was buried from the frame church."

In a number of his columns, Otto recalled the lives of the last native Ohlone to live here, a woman known only as "Maria." She had two sons, "Cache" and "Tahoe," who were apparently friends of Otto in his childhood and who he remembered as "two of the best baseball players in town." They also loved to watch the fire department at work. "Several fires mysteriously broke out during one training season," Otto wrote, "including the burning of the Imus barn on Potrero." The two boys were found guilty of setting the fires and were sent to prison. Otto captured the depths of the tragedy in three simple sentences:

> Cache was a coachman for Mrs. P.B. Fagan. While he was being held, the Fagan dog stayed faithfully outside the jail fence on High Street. Both boys were sent to San Quentin and died there.

Given his own ethnic background, Otto frequently noted the contributions of German immigrants to local history. In a series of five lengthy columns published posthumously during the winter of 1957, Otto focused on the activities of immigrant German businessmen in the Santa Cruz area, particularly Claus Spreckels and Frederick A. Hihn. Spreckels, of course, first developed the sugarbeet industry near Aptos, while Hihn developed the first Santa Cruz-Watsonville railroad, subdivided Capitola, and made a fortune in lumber. Otto also wrote occasional columns about the Scottish, Irish and French living in Santa Cruz, but what is truly his most significant and most unique contribution to the annals of local history is the writing he did on the Chinese. Almost all we know about the early Santa Cruz Chinatowns is derived from Otto's recollections of his childhood jaunts there. As Sandy Lydon notes in *Chinese Gold: The Chinese in the Monterey Bay Region,* reading Otto's columns "is like visiting Santa Cruz in the 1880s in the company of an anthropologist who sees everything from table height ...The Santa Cruz Chinese had no greater friend than Ernest Otto, and it is as if the spirits placed him there to balance the strident defamation that had been written earlier." Lydon is referring to the decades of anti-Chinese rhetoric which appeared in the pages of Santa Cruz newspapers during the late 19th Century, the most vehement of which was written by Duncan McPherson, editor and publisher of the *Sentinel.* Lydon further notes the additional irony of Otto's laudatory pieces on the Chinese appearing decades later in the same paper operated by McPherson.

Two factors clearly played a critical role in Otto's early association with the Chinese: his youth and his religion. As a boy, Otto was able to slip beneath the social barriers which separated the Chinese community from the larger white society. Otto was raised during the height of a vigilant anti-Chinese movement in Santa Cruz, and few adults would have had the courage to stand up against the tide of public sentiment and befriend the Chinese. (It should be recalled that the anti-Chinese referendum of 1879 passed in Santa Cruz County by a margin of 2,450 to 4.) On the other hand, a young white boy wandering through Chinatown was no threat to the Chinese; had Otto been older during this era, he might not have been so warmly welcomed.

Otto's continued relationship with the Chinese was also abetted by his membership in the First Congregational Church, which operated a "mission" in the Santa Cruz Chinatown. Otto was actively involved with all aspects of the church, including the Chinese mission, and always attended its annual recitals during the spring. "The members sang gospel hymns in Chinese and English," Otto recalled, "and passed sweetmeats to visitors."

Fellow Congregational Church member Duncan McPherson took a dimmer view of such proceedings, urging the "Celestials... to return to the land of their nativity." Otto, who believed in practicing the tolerance preached in the Bible, no doubt bristled at McPherson's remarks. Years later, in the 83rd Anniversary Edition of the *Sentinel,* Otto concluded his piece by noting: "I could tell of the sufferings of the patient Chinese who were the target... of the slogan in vogue for a number of years: 'The Chinese Must Go.'"

While Otto certainly sympathized with those sufferings, he rarely referred to them in his writings and chose instead to paint a rich and detailed cultural portrait of life inside the Santa Cruz Chinatown. He wrote literally dozens of columns on the Chinese over the years, and while some of them are repetitive, taken together they constitute a colorful and textured historical mosaic. Otto wrote about Chinese laundries, religious temples, newspapers, vegetable vendors, eating habits, fish dryers, barbers, New Year's celebrations, and other cultural practices. His accounts of numerous Chinese funerals provide a vivid remembrance of those unique and ornate rituals:

> Two days before the ceremonial, a large Chinese delivery basket was before the place where he lived and scores came and each left a package of incense, red candles, imitation paper money and paper clothes were dropped in the basket and all burned later at the cemetery. A large platform or altar was erected in the street and tall punks and candles were burning. On the platform was a huge roast porker and also there was an unroasted goat, one skinned. There were roast chickens and other food. Chinese approached before the improvised altar and burned punks, red candles, imitation money and clothes useable in the next world. Kneeling on strips of white matting, they burned their offerings and from a pewter pot poured libations of wine.

Otto was especially taken as a young boy by the common practice of opium smoking (he claimed that "over half" of the Chinese living here in the 1890s engaged in the activity). Otto was apparently allowed free rein of the opium dens, which he often visited while delivering letters or newspapers.

> We used to watch with interest as the smoker took the long needle, placed it in the receptacle and twisted the opium around it. He would hold the opium over the flame and it would begin to bubble. It would form a ball and the smoker would place the ball in the center of the bowl of his pipe and inhale the smoke. As we boys watched, he would come under the influence of the drug and soon would be asleep, enjoying, we felt sure, wonderful dreams.

The Chinese were Otto's friends and, in spite of their continued social ostracism from mainstream society, he afforded them the same respect and courtesy at the time of their deaths that he afforded all other Santa Cruzans. Their obituaries were almost always lengthy accounts, and Otto strove to include details about their lives which acknowledged their roles in the community. When one of the last of the early-day Santa Cruz Chinese, Chin Lai, passed away in March 1949, Otto noted the various lumber camps he had worked in as a cook and that he had also been a vegetable vendor. He included details about his religious practices and his style of dress. "Of late, his head was usually covered with a tight felt cap with no brim," Otto wrote. "Usually he was smoking one of the old time Chinese pipes with a tiny brass bowl." Even in his obituaries, no detail was too small.

Perhaps the one surprising omission in Otto's historical writings on Santa Cruz is the absence of the Genovese-Italians in any of his columns. As was noted earlier, he wrote about them considerably in his "Waterfront" reports, but there is absolutely no mention in Otto's historical work of their role in establishing the commercial fisheries here. Perhaps their community remained too vibrant, too active, for Otto to pigeon-hole them into the quietude of the past; in any event, he never did.

When Ernest Otto died in July 1955, he left a backlog of "Old Santa Cruz" columns so large that the *Sentinel* continued running them some two years after his death. Given the flow of some of the columns, it seemed likely that he wrote sequences of them in single sittings. It also might seem that he was intending to include them as chapters in a book, although those who knew him discount this theory. He was too much of a daily newspaperman to ever write an extended volume; they argue he was probably just building up a backlog of newspaper copy for a rainy day.

Otto's death on July 10 truly cast a dark cloud over the Santa Cruz community. Thousands came to pay tribute to the man who had given them news and history for over 70 years and who had made an indelible mark on the city of his birth.

Fred McPherson, Jr., then editor and publisher of the *Sentinel*, noted that "loyalty was the keynote to (his) character," while Malio Stagnaro, dean of the Santa Cruz fishing fleet, said, "The whole waterfront has lost a great friend. Words cannot express our sorrow. He was not only a friend to us on the wharf, but to everyone in Santa Cruz. The title 'Mr. Santa Cruz' truly fits him." On the day of his funeral, a prophetic editorial in the *Sentinel* put it best: "The echo of his footsteps on his beloved waterfront is gone, but years from now, there will still be legends of Ernest Otto, a man blessed by God."

—1988

FREDDY ALNAS:
Santa Cruz Is in the Heart

THE FIRST LOW TIDE OF the day follows closely on the heels of dawn, and Freddy Alnas, a bucket and iron cane in one hand, a well-worn pocket knife in the other, is busy scuttling about the tide pools of Lighthouse Point in search of seaweed for his evening meal. He leans over and, just as he might have a half-century ago on the other side of the earth, carefully slices a small bunch of kelp from a rock and places it in the bucket with the rest of his harvest. "That good seaweed," he says in an English that is richly colored by both Spanish and the dialect of his native Luzon Island in the northern Philippines. "Chinese like it. Make good soup."

Droplets of saltwater sparkle on his thick, tawny hands as he lifts himself upright with the aid of his cane. "Good spot over there," he points, and slowly he is moving towards more bounty, very much at ease here among the hermit crabs and young surfers in pursuit of other sensations at Steamer Lane.

Later, his bucket full, Freddy hunts for pile worms along the cliffs. He will use them for bait in a few hours when the tide is higher and schools of fish move into the small, rocky coves three or four miles up the coast. Fishing is good, and by the time the wind picks up in the late afternoon, Freddy has a nice string of perch. He cleans the fish, then the seaweed, packs everything neatly into the trunk of his faded blue Ford, and drives to his apartment at a senior and low-income housing project on the west side of town.

Freddy moves easily about his kitchen. For over 30 years he worked intermittently as a cook in the Filipino farm labor camps north of Santa Cruz. Very quickly, the fish and seaweed join with some steamed rice to form a meal more truly suited for the gods. "Eat, eat!" Freddy urges his guests. "There plenty fish." His eyes are smiling as his friends enjoy the fruits of his many labors. He reaches down at his own plate, rolls some rice and seaweed into a ball, and pushes it into his mouth.

In many ways, Freddy's life story embodies the dark side of Santa Cruz County history. At one time there were up to 2500 Filipino men living here, and it was largely their labor which turned the soils of the Pajaro Valley and north coast into the fertile farm lands they are today. It is a story long buried in our county's history. But it still burns in the hearts of the men who lived it.

In 1930, 17-year-old Freddy Alnas, weak and sickly from a near-fatal case of the mumps, left his mother and three sisters in the Philippines for the promise of wealth in California. His father, a rice farmer in Luzon who worked his paddies with a plow pulled by caribou, had left the impoverished islands a year earlier and found work in the lettuce fields near San Juan Bautista. Freddy joined his father, two uncles and some cousins on lettuce crews up and down the Salinas and Pajaro Valleys.

Between 1924, the year of the Japanese Immigration Act, which prohibited the further entrance of Japanese laborers into the U.S., and 1930, 35,000 Filipinos arrived in California to replace Japanese workers in the fields. Almost all of them were men, and like their counterparts in San Francisco's Chinatown, theirs was a bachelor's society, a society in which marriage was foreign, and gambling, drinking and dance hall girls were all a part of the daily routine. "The women never left," says Freddy. "Stay in Philippines and take care of home." In California, the ratio of Filipino men to women was 14 to 1.

Discriminatory practices against the new arrivals were abundant. Filipinos were barred from hotels, cafés, swimming pools, barbershops, pool halls and most neighborhoods. Forced to live in rundown apartments, they often packed a dozen friends and relatives into a single room. They were also, of course, prohibited from marrying white women: California's anti-miscegenation law, first passed in 1872 and amended in 1906, forbade all interracial marriages and was not repealed until 1948. "To be a Filipino in California," observed the late Carey McWilliams in *Brothers Under the Skin,* "is to belong to a blood brotherhood, a freemasonry of the ostracized... Their own native cultural values have been cast aside, yet at the same time, an uncrossable chasm exists between them and American life."

Though it has never been known for its racial tolerance, the city of Watsonville found itself at the social center of a large Filipino community. Tension between whites and Filipinos had been mounting in South County throughout the late Twenties. With the growing economic strains and resultant unemployment brought on by the Great Depression, that tension snapped during an ugly two-week period the year of Freddy's arrival.

The Watsonville Anti-Filipino Riot of 1930, a piece of local history that was to have national—and international—repercussions, was precipitated, as Freddy remembers, largely by the presence of white women who danced with Filipinos for pay at a Pinoy nightclub between Watsonville and Moss Landing.

Racist rhetoric by both a Monterey County judge and the Watsonville *Evening Pajaronian* fueled anti-Filipino sentiment. During the week of January 10, the *Evening Pajaronian* distinguished itself with a series of inflammatory articles and headlines intended to stir up vigilante activities. The paper, for instance, saw fit to feature the opinions of a local socialite, who declared, "Taxi-dance halls where white women dance with Orientals may be all right in San Francisco or Los Angeles, but not in our community. We won't stand for anything of the kind." Almost immediately thereafter, five days of rioting broke out in the greater Watsonville area. Angry mobs of whites, ranging in number from 200 to 700, sought out Filipinos in the streets, bars, farms and field houses. On the final day of the rioting, 700 vigilantes chased 46 Filipinos down Watsonville's Main Street, where they were fortunate enough to find refuge and police protection in the city council chambers.

Frustrated within the city limits, the mob dispersed and headed for the farmlands. Near the John Murphy Ranch on San Juan Road, just a few miles from the Alnas family camp, a carload of young men sprayed bullets into a Filipino bunkhouse. Fermin Tobera, 22, was shot through the heart and killed instantly. Although a good deal of evidence was gathered which pointed directly at a suspect, Edsel Frey, no one was ever prosecuted for the murder.

"Them boys jealous we with white girls," Freddy recalls. "They hit us, use tear gas. They make threats, but we stay." Others, however, were not as hardy as the Alnas clan, and many Watsonville Filipinos scattered to cities where they received warmer welcomes.

In spite of the prejudices they faced, Freddy and his father soon saved enough money to purchase a late-model Chevy sedan. Sometimes work on a particular farm would only take a few hours, leaving the field hands stranded and unemployed for the rest of the day. "With car," says Freddy, "six guys, maybe more, can move around from field to field. Pretty crowded. You got to put your Army bags and blankets on the running boards, on the bumpers. Drive that way all the time." One day they might be in King City, the next, back in Watsonville.

Freddy developed a pattern where he would work in the lettuce fields in the spring and early summer, then travel up to Alaska for four or five weeks of employment in the salmon canneries, and finally, return to Stockton to harvest asparagus. The latter, according to Freddy, was the most difficult. "Asparagus very hard. You walk all day in soft, dusty soil. Bad on legs. Guys tired when winter comes."

Given the often wretched conditions under which they worked and the strong bonds developed in their ethnic communities, it was not surprising that Filipinos formed some of the most successful unions in the history of California agriculture. Their first attempt was the Filipino Labor Union, founded in the early 1930s, followed later by the Filipino Agricultural Labor Association.

These organizations staged a number of important strikes—including the Salinas Lettuce Strikes of 1934 and 1936, and a major strike in the Brussels sprout fields of northern Santa Cruz County in 1960—and it was a group of Filipinos (not Hispanics, as is commonly thought) who initiated the Delano Grape Strike of 1965, which first brought national attention to Cesar Chavez and his fledgling United Farm Workers' Association.

Freddy was a participant in much of this labor history, including the notorious 1934 Salinas strike in which Filipinos joined mostly white members of the Vegetable Packers' Association (VPA) in demanding higher wages from lettuce growers. The Filipinos were asking for a 15-cent-an-hour raise (from 30 to 45 cents), while VPA members were seeking nearly twice that much.

When the growers gave in to the demands of the VPA, the packers responded by turning their backs on the Filipinos, who were then subjected to vigilante attacks aimed at breaking their strike. Those strong-arm tactics proved successful, as Filipinos returned to the fields with a token five-cent-an-hour raise. "That pay still too low," remembers Freddy. "White guys scare us into strike, threaten us with bombs, then break their word."

Freddy continued to follow crops up and down California—peas in Pescadero, grapes in Delano, winter lettuce in the Imperial Valley. Then in 1942, world events pulled Freddy and his friends from the fields. Following the bombing of Pearl Harbor, Franklin Roosevelt signed an executive proclamation which allowed Filipinos to enlist in the armed forces, and Freddy joined the Air Force's 46th Fighting Squadron in Iwo Jima. While in Hawaii completing basic training, Freddy received his U.S. citizenship.

"I was very happy to be American citizen," he recalls. "I glad to go fight Japanese. They invaded the Philippines too. Kill many people." In 1945 he was granted an honorable discharge as a sergeant.

After the war, Freddy returned to field work. He took a job as a cook on one of the Brussels sprout farms near Davenport, from where he journeyed as far east as New Mexico and Texas in the off-season. It was while picking lettuce near Albuquerque that Freddy contracted *coccidioidomycosis*, more commonly referred to as "valley fever," a fungus which attaches itself to the lung. Spores of this disease reside just below the surface of the soil and are disrupted during periods of cultivation. They reach their victims on particles of dust, leaving field workers especially susceptible to the disease.

The cure for valley fever is lengthy and painful. Freddy spent 14 months in a San Francisco hospital recuperating. While bedridden, circulatory problems developed in his left knee. That condition resulted in four more operations, a permanently stiff leg, and, as recently as a year ago, the threat of amputation.

But the life of Freddy Alnas was not, as they say, all work and no play. To see his smile is to know that he is a man who enjoys a good time, a few drinks perhaps, a night on the town. There are photos of him on the dresser proudly escorting beautiful women. If you press him hard enough, he will confess that yes, he was something of a ladies' man, though like most Filipinos who came here, he never married.

The great passion of Freddy's life, however, was not to be found in nightclubs. Cockfights were a central component of Filipino culture, a regular diversion from the day-to-day rigor of the fields. Huge crowds would gather on the ranches near the Filipino bunkhouses in order to watch the fights and place bets. A five-inch blade was secured to the left leg of the fighting roosters, and they were placed in a small circular area where they fought until one of them was killed. "Guys bet plenty," Freddy smiles. "Sometimes $400."

Freddy owned a number of fighting cocks and developed a reputation as an excellent trainer. "His roosters were always top fighters," remembers a friend. "That's why we call him 'Freddy Number One.' I won lots of money betting on Freddy."

As a cook, Freddy had special control over his roosters' diets, a steady supply of whole corn soaked in water. "You have to take good care of them, massage them, feed them good. Always raise two at a time—just in case."

Sometimes the losers wound up in the soup kettle, but not Freddy's. "I bury mine. Cook them for an hour and they still too tough."

Local law enforcement agencies began to crack down on the practice in the 1950s. After a few arrests, Freddy decided to give up the fights. "Some guy called me not too long ago," says Freddy. "Ask me to come see fight. I say no. Don't want to pay no more fines."

Freddy spends most of his time these days fishing, gardening and cooking for his roommate and lifelong friend, Petacio Balando. The majority of his other friends and cousins still live in the old bachelor communities of San Juan Bautista, Watsonville and the north coast. Freddy always seems to be delivering gifts of fish, vegetables, seaweed or sweet rice in one of these locales.

"If Freddy thinks you're hungry," says one of his neighbors, "he's bound to get you something to eat. And there's no one in their right mind who would turn him down. That man is a master in the kitchen."

When Freddy retired in 1981, after more than 50 years of work in the fields and cookhouses, there was no celebration, no gold watch, no commendation to hang above his mantel. A bum leg and a bum lung were the tangible rewards of his 50-year service.

"Do you know what a Filipino feels like in America?" wrote the poet Carlos Buloson, whose autobiographical *America Is in the Heart* is the classic piece of literature on the Filipino-American experience. "He is the loneliest thing on earth. There is much to be appreciated all about him, beauty, wealth, grandeur, power. But is he a part of these luxuries? He looks, poor man, through the fingers of his eyes. He is enchained, damnably to his race, his heritage. He is betrayed."

And that is at least half of the truth. The American Dream was never really Freddy's to reach for; it was always beyond his grasp. His labor was good enough to keep him in America, but never enough to make him a part of it.

But if the plastic grandeur and the silicon luxuries were never his, Freddy was afforded other beauties. With all respect to Buloson, we should not confuse simplicity with poverty, nor convenience with wealth. If Freddy is bitter about his lot, he certainly does not show it.

During an era when most of us are punched into time clocks, Freddy's life is still guided by the coming and going of the tides, changes in wind patterns, ocean currents and the seasons. He is freed by his labors, not enslaved by them, and that which we regularly overlook is likely to be a central part of his daily existence.

Freddy came to California over 50 years ago with every intention of returning to the Philippines—of returning with enough money to secure a comfortable life for himself and family. But like most of the 35,000 Filipinos who migrated here in the 1920s, a permanent return was never made. They settled up and down the California coast, most remaining bachelors, a few starting families well into their 40s and early 50s.

According to the 1980 Census, there are 357,000 Filipinos living in California (many of whom came in the last decade, fleeing the terror of the Marcos regime), and they now constitute the largest Asian ethnic group in the state.

Freddy himself has returned to the land of his birth twice for short visits, once in 1945 and again in 1970, when he built his youngest sister a home on the family plot he left as a youth. Well into his 70s, he is surprisingly ambivalent about returning for a last time.

"If I go back, my family there want this and that because I come from America. They want too much," he says. There is an uncharacteristic scowl on his face as he makes these remarks, maybe even a trace of resentment. His hands are busy stretching out some fresh fish on a drying rack, when suddenly, the smile returns. "Besides, I like it here. Good place. Plenty friends. Plenty to eat too."

—1983

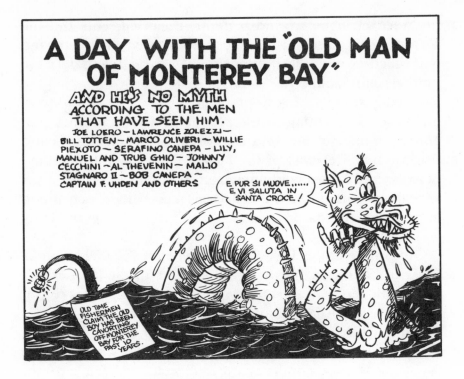

THE OLD MAN OF MONTEREY BAY

WHEN SANTA CRUZ FISHERMAN Bill Totten returned to the docks after a day of fishing in June of 1941, he was badly shaken. "I saw that serpent or monster out there," he screamed. "Get me out of here. I'm going home."

"He was scared to death," recalled the late Italian fishing patriarch Malio Stagnaro, who greeted Totten at the docks that afternoon. "He must have seen something. I didn't see him around the wharf for a while."

Totten was the last of a long series of local fishermen who claimed to have seen a large serpent off the Santa Cruz coast. The huge serpent or sea monster, usually sighted in the waters of the mile-deep Monterey Canyon, was affectionately referred to as the "Old Man of Monterey Bay."

"Yeah, I saw it when I was a kid," declares veteran fisherman Victor Ghio, whose brother Lily and uncles Manuel and Trub Ghio also saw the beast in the 1930s. "We didn't know it then, but it was probably a big elephant seal or walrus. Something like that."

Others who saw the monster included Joe Loero, Marco Olivieri, Willie Piexoto, Serafino Canepa, Al Thevenin, "Stago" Stagnaro and Robby Canepa. The beast was usually described as looking like a sea-going dragon, with a huge head, long tail and spines along its back—though no one ever got a picture of it.

In 1942 the San Francisco *Call Bulletin*'s famed cartoonist Tommy Thompson drafted a sketch of the monster based on a variety of descriptions. Presumably, the bifocals and toothpick he included in the drawing were added for comic relief.

While many land-lovers attributed the sightings to the need for psychological relief brought about by the hardships of the Great Depression, an unusual discovery that occurred in the spring of 1925 lends more than a little credence to the fishermen's claims.

On June 1 of that year, Charles Moore journeyed down to his beach a few miles north of Santa Cruz to find a 37- foot beast washed up on shore. No one was quite sure what it was.

The day after Moore's discovery, the Santa Cruz *Sentinel* described the creature as having "a tail something like that of a whale and a mammoth head with a mouth like the bill of a duck." According to Randall Reinstedt's delightful book, *Mysterious Sea Monsters of the Central Coast,* other descriptions included "elephant-like legs" and "ivory toenails."

Dr. David Starr Jordan, president emeritus of Stanford University, classified the rapidly decomposing carcass as a "bottle-nosed porpoise," while E.L. Wallace, twice president of the Natural History Society of British Columbia, thought it to be a prehistoric "Plesiosarus" that had been preserved in an Arctic glacier and subsequently dislodged into the sea through centuries of glacial melting.

Following a few more days of speculation, the California Academy of Sciences took over the classification process, declaring that the beast was actually a beaked whale, so rare that it had only a Latin name, Berardius bairdi. "No one has been able to name it positively," the *Sentinel* wryly observed after a week of squabbling, "but when it comes to smell, all are of one mind." The skull of the Moore's Beach creature is now housed under lock and key in the California Academy's Steinhart Aquarium in San Francisco.

—1985

Louis Venable, Pacific Avenue, 1919.

BEYOND LOUDEN NELSON:
Black History In Santa Cruz

THE YEAR IS 1951—the scene, Winkle Avenue, near the present site of the Skyview Drive-in Theater. Reverend William Brent, pastor of the Santa Cruz Missionary Baptist Church, has just purchased a small, comfortable home there so that he can move his family down from San Francisco.

On Saturday night, November 3, the day after Brent completed his purchase, a fire broke out in his newly bought home, completely destroying the kitchen and pantry and causing smoke damage to the remainder of the living quarters.

At that time, Santa Cruz's black community was confined almost exclusively to the "Circles" neighborhood on the west side of the city, and Brent's decision to locate outside of those confines represented a bold effort on his behalf to break the city's segregated housing pattern.

The day after the fire, as Brent surveyed the damage to his home, a score of white residents appeared on his lawn, demanding to speak to him. "They told me this is a white community and they wanted to keep it that way," Brent later told police. They told me that if I came back, there would be more damage to the house similar to the fire if I still tried moving into the neighborhood."

The mob of white residents also offered to pay back the $300 he put down on the home if he promised to abandon his hopes of moving there. "They were angry," Brent noted, "and they meant business."

Although a state investigator concluded that the blaze was intentionally set by an arsonist, no one was ever arrested for the incident. Brent and his family later moved back to San Francisco.

Anyone trying to get a full sense of black history in Santa Cruz will be sadly disappointed by the paucity of material on the subject. Margaret Koch's widely sold history of the county, *Parade of the Past*, for instance, devotes all of seven sentences to black history here, and the story of the Brent incident—and others like it—are nowhere to be found in those pages. The one published work on local black history, a thin pamphlet called "The History of the Santa Cruz County NAACP," by Kreta Graves-Gray, provides a wonderful introduction to the local chapter of the civil rights organization and a general overview of race relations here, but it stands conspicuously alone, with nothing to augment it.

The great exception to this neglect, of course, are all the obligatory references to Louden ("London") Nelson, after whom the city's community center was named in 1979. As just about everyone who has lived here for any length of time knows only too well, Nelson was a former slave—probably from North Carolina or Tennessee—who arrived in Santa Cruz in

1848. A cobbler and gardener, he died in 1860, leaving his entire estate "to the children of Santa Cruz" in order to help further their education. The present city school board's offices are located on some of the land he left to the city.

While Nelson's contribution to Santa Cruz history is certainly worthy of the special attention it has received, the subsequent chapters of local black history remain an enigma, a forgotten chronicle of life, death and spirit lost forever to the ages.

There are many reasons for this vacuum, not the least of which is the simple fact that until the end of World War II, there were never many blacks who lived here, and certainly never anything that amounted to a viable black community. Nonetheless, there was a small trickle of a black population here beginning with the period of Reconstruction, and we only have the slightest sense of what life here was like for them.

The historical notes of Rowland and Ernest Otto record the existence of a barber named Joe Smallwood, a bootblack named George Chester, and a cooper's apprentice known only as "Old Joe," who, Otto recalled, "wore his hair braided in twists that stood out several inches from his head."

All of them, presumably, remained here until their deaths, but there was also a young black man living here during the 1880s who did not stay. Joseph Francis graduated with highest honors from Santa Cruz High and left for San Francisco, where he became a widely respected editor of a weekly black newspaper and a clerk with the Southern Pacific Railroad. He never came back to Santa Cruz.

There was good reason not to come back. A rigid, often repressive, Protestant community, Santa Cruz was never particularly open to outsiders who didn't fit the WASP mold. During the 1920s, the Ku Klux Klan established a strong foothold here, creating an atmosphere something akin to the deep south.

In the aftermath of World War II, however, with California's black population swelling to 400,000, the first substantial black community was established in Santa Cruz. The center of that community was Reverend Brent's Baptist Church, located then on Branciforte Avenue and later on Woodrow, and it remains the center of that particular community into the 1980s.

While the history of that church has never been written, a former UCSC American Studies student, Jessica Friedman, conducted a series of interviews there in 1986 which provide the beginnings of a rich and powerful historical tale.

One of Friedman's interviews was with Isaac Jackson, head deacon of the church for 33 years. During World War II, Jackson recalled, "my company in the army was all black, with a few white officers. I came here in '42...there was 15 blacks here, that's what you had. Most of the people you see here now have only been here the last 30 years. It was a ghost town when I arrived."

The stories recall the struggles and triumphs of a black community isolated from the white mainstream. Virtually all confirm an agony of trying to live here in a sea of subtle racism, where casual slights were often more devastating than more blatant acts and remarks. It is a history which has repeated itself all too often in this city of the Holy Cross—and it continues to repeat itself to this day.

—1986

ATOP THE GOLDEN MOUNTAIN:
The Ow Family of Santa Cruz

IN THE SPRING WHEN THE willows and chickens grew fat again and the plum trees blossomed pink and white in the Chinatown yards near the river, the old man with the scruffy beard and tobacco breath sat back in the quiet splendor of the warm April sun and watched with great delight the group of young children playing at his feet.

Far off in the distance, he could hear the children's grandmother, Lee Gue She, turning over the soil of her garden and the San Lorenzo River tumbling gently through the town. He could smell the fish drying on the porches and the herbs from the kitchens and the faint, sweet wisps of Chinese tobacco in the air. The world had changed many times in his life, he thought as he watched the scene unfolding before him, and it would change many times more after he was gone.

Chin Lai closed his eyes and felt the sun on his face. Another old Chinese man, Ah Fook, hurried by carrying a gunny sack full of fish he had just caught on his daily journey to the wharf. Still another, Moon Lai Bok, carried a load of stovewood on his back. The children watched the old men amble along the gravel road as they played.

One of them, 4-year-old George Ow, Jr., climbed up into the warm comfort of Chin Lai's lap. He always felt safe there, far away from the outside world where his people were still all-too-often called "chinks" and "slant-eyes." The old men always protected him and showered him with love, and he reserved for them his greatest respect and admiration.

Born nearly a century before in the days of the Manchu Dynasty, the old men had left their villages and had come to America—Gum Shan, the land of "the Golden Mountain"—in pursuit of wealth and riches; they had found instead poverty and racism. Anti-miscegenation laws prevented them from marrying white women, and immigration restrictions prevented Chinese women from joining them in the States. They had helped build California's railroads and developed the state's fisheries and agriculture, but in return, they were forced to live as aging bachelors on the fringes of the dominant white society.

Young George Ow, Jr., didn't know the history of his Chinese elders as he sat in Chin Lai's lap. What he did know was that the old men were his unofficial uncles, who gave him candy and firecrackers and told him funny stories in their native Cantonese dialect. He knew that most of them lived together in the dark, musty Chee Kong Tong temple, with its sticks of incense burning, colorful flags and pictures of Sun Yat-sen, Chiang Kai-shek and Abraham Lincoln on the walls. That they were always close was all that mattered.

It was the spring of 1947 and Santa Cruz's aging, ramshackle Chinatown was a happy place for a young boy to be growing up. All about him, new life seemed to be singing everywhere.

In less than a decade, however, Chin Lai, Ah Fook and Moon Lai Bok would be dead, and the Santa Cruz Chinatown would be dead, too. No longer would the plum trees blossom in springtime, nor the chickens grow plump and sassy—and young George Ow, Jr., and his family would be living in Monterey.

Long before the final days of the Santa Cruz Chinatown, a young man from the Canton region of China journeyed to the United States to seek work and wealth, and to escape the poverty of his native land. He was George Ow, Jr.'s grandfather, Lam Pon, and he came to the U.S. before the turn of the century as a so-called "merchant" to side-step the Chinese Immigration Act which prohibited the immigration of Chinese laborers to the U.S. after 1882. Like many of his fellow countrymen, it is believed he worked on the railroads when he first arrived. Later, Lam Pon worked as a cook and laundryman. Eventually, he arrived in Santa Cruz, home to a small, though somewhat thriving Chinese community, and he found work as a cook at the Riverside Hotel, which was then run by the Barson family.

In 1905, notes Sandy Lydon's *Chinese Gold*, "Lam Pon entered a lease agreement with Ralph J. Mattison of Aptos and built a two-chimney apple dryer on the field behind the Bay View Hotel. Each fall, Lam Pon moved to a small house near the dryer in Aptos, while several dozen Chinese moved into the bunkhouse adjacent to the dryer. By 1910, Lam Pon was secure enough in his business to consider marriage to a young California-born Chinese woman from Pleasanton, California." Her name was Ow Shee.

By the 1920s, Lam Pon expanded his business base by opening the first Chinese restaurant in Santa Cruz and a small Chinatown bank. The Lam's eldest daughter, Anna, was born in 1912, and a son, George, in 1921.

Anna (Lam) Liu remembers her father, Lam Pon, as a stern man with a great deal of drive and discipline. She recalls her mother, Ow Shee, as being "very traditional"; although born in the U.S., Ow Shee had returned to China at the age of five to receive a traditional Chinese upbringing. "She never learned to speak English," Liu notes. "It was as if she were born back there. The only thing was that she was an American citizen, so she was entitled to come back. Her marriage to my father was arranged—every bit of it."

Liu, herself, began attending grammar school in Aptos during the 1920s. One particular incident sticks out in her memory. "When I first started school I was very, very shy," she says, "because I didn't have much outside contact, you know. There weren't many Chinese, and, of course, other people didn't associate with us. The first couple of days there was this rowdy boy, and he threw rocks at me. I started crying and went to my dad, and he went down to the school and told the teacher. Well, the boy got reprimanded and after that he didn't do it anymore!"

During the apple drying season, the Lam family would reside in Aptos, then return to Santa Cruz Chinatown for the remainder of the year. While her father was able to come and go as he pleased, Liu remembers that her mother was "a prisoner of the house. . . The farthest she could go was maybe a few blocks away, and even that would cause a stir among the old men who lived there."

While Lam Pon was not constrained by his gender, he continued to feel restrained by the anti-Chinese laws and public sentiments which were still very much extant in the U.S. During the 1920s, he and his family had traveled back and forth to China (on one such journey his son, George, was born), and even though he was a successful businessman, by 1930 he had decided to return permanently to his home in China. "He was a proud man and had been financially successful," says his son, George Ow, Sr., "but like most Chinese in America at that time, he still felt a certain amount of discrimination. He couldn't go into many restaurants and most barbers wouldn't cut his hair. And he couldn't buy property or become a citizen. In other words, he couldn't fully enjoy his prosperity, so he went back to China."

During the 1930s, China was a world waiting to be transformed. The once quiet, feudal nation was on the verge of being caught in a vortex of internal revolution and international conflict. In 1937, as the Japanese were invading Shanghai, miles to the north of Canton, Lam Pon saw the writing on the wall. The China of the '30s was no longer the China of his youth; it was a place of little opportunity and seemingly no future, particularly for young men and women with business aspirations. Lam Pon had made his peace with his homeland, but his son, he decided, should return to the land of the Gold Mountain. It would be safer there and there would be economic opportunities as well.

By that time, Lam Pon's daughter, Anna, had been married a year and had a child. For her own safety, she and her family moved to Hong Kong. Her mother, Ow Shee, also joined them, and together they saw 16-year-old George depart on his journey to America.

Ow's oceanic journey to the U.S. was not without its dramas. Just out of dock, his passenger ship, the U.S.S. President Hoover, was mistaken by Chinese war planes as a Japanese troop ship and was hit by a bomb on the deck. "It just killed one man," Ow recalls, "and we were able to limp into San Francisco."

The Chinese Exclusion Act, of course, still severely restricted immigration to the U.S. Using his American-born mother's family name, "George Ow" was able to make his way quickly through the bureaucratic nightmare at the Angel Island Immigration Center in San Francisco Bay.

In strict terms of the law, Ow was an illegal alien. Although his mother was indeed a native-born American, she had lost her citizenship when she married a non-citizen, Lam Pon. He was thus a "paper angel," claiming to be the son of his mother's brother living in Arizona.

George Ow, Sr., arrived in the City of St. Francis with two American dollars in his pocket, a strong will, and the name of an uncle, Lam Sing, who lived in Santa Cruz.

Lam Sing was the younger brother of Lam Pon, and his Chinese grocery store, the Canton Market, served an important social function for young Chinese immigrants in the Monterey Bay area during the dark days of the Depression. Not only did it provide a place of employment, but it also served as a rooming house and gathering spot where the Cantonese dialect was the predominant language. It was the cool corner of the melting pot.

Ow, Sr., began working at the market as soon as he arrived. For a few hours a day, Lam Sing allowed him to take courses at Santa Cruz High School, where he studied English, math and business. One of his classmates was his brother-in-law to be, George Lee. Another was Gilda Stagnaro, of the Italian fishing family, who remembers him as a "hard-working, dutiful student."

"It was pretty difficult," Ow recalls of his early days at Santa Cruz High, "because coming from China, you didn't understand the language, and it was very frustrating. I couldn't learn as fast as I wanted to, but everyone was very kind to me—the students and the teachers—and gradually I picked it up." He received his high school diploma in 1940.

After working seven days a week and putting in up to 14-hour days when he wasn't in school, Ow decided it was time for a change of scenery. He decided to do a little traveling and worked his way through Southern California and then back north again. "I worked on farms, in restaurants and grocery stores. I was able to roam around the country and see what America was like." It was a cultural education for Ow, and he kept copious mental notes on the manners, habits and customs of his new homeland. He spent two years on his journey before he began to "get lonely." He returned to Santa Cruz and found work at the apple drying operation in Aptos that was founded by his father and which was still being run by his distant cousin, Otto Lam.

Changes, however, were once again imminent. The Pacific war, which the 16-year-old boy from Canton had sought to escape, crossed the ocean in December of 1941, and by 1942, it had caught up with him. After Pearl Harbor, Ow was drafted into the U.S. Army, but not before marrying a young Santa Cruz woman he had taken a fancy to, Emily Lee. They were married in February of 1942.

By the beginning of the Second World War, only a few families were still residing in the Santa Cruz Chinatown, one of which was the clan of Sung Sai Lee and Gue She Lee. Sung Sai Lee was born in the village of Sien Toon, China, in 1881. His father was of the generation of Chinese men that had come to the U.S. to build the railroads, and near the turn of the century, Sung Sai himself journeyed to the U.S. for seven years. In 1919, well after his first wife had died, Sung Sai married a young woman from the neighboring village of Heang Sun. Her given name was Han Thein, meaning "a heart of no worry"; she was 19 years old at the time of her marriage and assumed the married name of Gue She Lee.

Three years later, Sung Sai Lee decided it was time for him and his wife to return to the U.S., or "the good land," as he called it. Because his father had been to America, Sung Sai was able to claim citizenship for himself and his wife. The couple left China by boat in October 1922, with Gue She seven months pregnant.

Arriving in San Francisco three weeks later, the Lees set up home in a small apartment on Stockton Street in San Francisco's Chinatown. Their first son, George, was born in December. Their first daughter, Emily, followed two years later.

In 1925, the Lees moved down to Santa Cruz, where they had often visited during the summers. They purchased a home on Bellevue Place in Chinatown, and Sung Sai was hired as a cook at the Wilder Dairy Ranch, a few miles north of Santa Cruz. It was a job he was to keep until the end of his life. He worked and stayed at the ranch six days a week, returning home on Sundays to visit his growing family.

The task of raising the family brood was thus left almost entirely to Gue She. Eventually she had seven children— George, Emily, Rose, Wee, Young, Luella and Jun— and they all were raised in the small, wood-framed home in the last Santa Cruz Chinatown.

Luella Lee Churchill remembers her mother as "an incredible woman . . . a really all-giving person. To have seven kids and have a husband living away from the home, it must have really been a struggle for her. And I don't ever remember her complaining. She just had a lot of courage."

Unlike the vast majority of Chinese immigrant women of her era, Gue She learned to speak English. Occasionally, she would venture out of Chinatown and shop at some of the downtown stores. But for the most part, her world was confined to her family, her home, and a large, thriving garden which she always kept to perfection. "She also raised rabbits," Luella remembers, "and she would butcher them and prepare them for us. And she had chickens, too. I remember she would sell the eggs to the neighbors for a little more shopping money. I mean, this woman did everything to raise her family."

During Chinese New Year, according to Emily (Lee) Ow, her mother would stay up long hours preparing special foods for the annual celebration. "I would wake up at nighttime and my mother would be making the Chinese dumplings and breads. At New Year's we always had plenty to eat. I don't think she had time to sleep."

As the older daughters, Emily and Rose assisted their mother in caring for the younger children, doing the housework, and also took on house cleaning jobs outside the home to augment the family income. Luella says that Emily was "like a second mother" to her. "For me, the youngest daughter, Emily was my first connection to life outside of Chinatown—she brought the outside world into the home. She made sure I had dresses and dolls—things my mom, given her background, couldn't have understood."

One thing which their mother insisted upon was that the Lee children receive an education. They all attended Laurel Elementary, Mission Hill and Santa Cruz High Schools. "We would never ever think about cutting school," Luella declares. "We were expected to go to school and do well, and that's what we did. She wouldn't have had it any other way."

On Sundays, Sung Sai Lee would return home from the Wilder Ranch for his one day with his family. He and Gue She would prepare a special meal on their wood-burning stove, and his seven children would gather around the table for their one dinner a week with their father. "He used to bring home tripe from the dairy ranch," says Emily, "and he'd make it into a tasty dish. And we'd always have chicken, too. We'd have this big meal and then go off to bed." By the time the children awoke the next morning, Sung Sai was on his way back to work at the ranch, ten miles away.

Life, at first, did not seem to change all that much for Emily Lee Ow after her marriage in February 1942. Her first child, George, Jr., was born in January of the following year, and so she went from taking care of her mother's youngest children to taking care of her own.

Across the ocean, in the Pacific campaign of World War II, George Ow, Sr., encountered the brutalities of war he had sought to escape as a 16-year-old in China. As a member of the Army's 40th Division, he was a part of the Guadalcanal campaign and the force that invaded the Philippines, then controlled by the Japanese. "There were a number of Chinese-Americans in the Philippine invasion force," Ow remembers. "I guess they figured that we hated the Japanese because they had invaded China. There was probably something to that because we won."

War-weary and ready to get on with a business career, Ow

returned to Santa Cruz in 1945. The family's second son, David, had been born a year earlier, and with two children, the Ows decided it was time to make a move.

Opportunity soon struck when some distant family members were selling a grocery store in Monterey for $3500. Ow, Sr., went to his uncle, Lam Sing, and asked for a loan. "The Chinese believed that 'the only way to get ahead is to go into business for yourself.' At that time, the average wage for Chinese was maybe $60 per month. There weren't a lot of opportunities, except in business. Lam Sing gave me the loan—no note, no nothing, just my word. That's the Chinese way."

So the Ows moved 40 miles south to Monterey, where they operated the New Monterey Market, just up from Cannery Row. "It was the typical old-style grocery store," Ow notes. "I cut the meat, and Emily took care of the grocery side and the register. We worked a good thirteen hours a day, seven days a week. When we ate lunch, maybe we'd take 10-15 minutes. They were tough days, but we did well. The canneries were going strong, and there was a lot of money from the war. If I remember right, I paid Lam Sing back within a year."

As Lydon notes in *Chinese Gold*, "The Ows succeeded in their market because they worked the edges. They had to compete with Safeway and Purity in New Monterey, but with their low overhead and flexibility, they worked around the chains, staying open later (usually to 11 p.m.) and on Sundays and holidays. Though they planned to work only a half-day on Christmas and Thanksgiving, it sometimes took most of the day to serve the customers who showed up at the store. The Ow children helped in the store after school, and the Ows would sometimes employ other Chinese in the community when they needed help."

By now the Ows had seven children. In addition to George, Jr. and David, there were Terry, Richard, Tom, Mary and Jeannee. All of the Ow kids helped out at the store, sorting bottles, bagging groceries, stocking, checking, and cleaning. Later on, the eldest son, George, Jr., was given the responsibility of handling bank transactions and opening and closing the store. They were all taught to be friendly to customers and to let them know they appreciated their business. The elder Ow's theory was that "someone who does not smile should not open a shop."

All the while, of course, Emily Ow was working double-time. Like her mother, she had seven children to care for and to make sure they were doing well in school, while at the same time, she still worked at the store, doing the bookkeeping, banking, and overseeing the ordering. It was a 365-day-a-year job.

In 1960, the Ows were hit with some unexpected competition. A Chinese family from Visalia built the Monterey Peninsula's first true supermarket, Monte Mart, only three blocks from the Ows. Although still able to hold their own financially, the Ows knew that another move was in order. Two years later, it came.

George Ow, Sr., had been fascinated by business ever since he was a young boy watching his father, Lam Pon, and he was an avid reader of business journals. In one such journal, he read a story that indicated that the most valuable commercial property in any given locale was that at the first major intersection off a freeway cloverleaf. Ow searched Monterey, Salinas and San Jose for such a property, but the land was either unavailable or too expensive. Finally, he turned to Santa Cruz and found just the piece he was looking for at the corner of 41st Avenue and Capitola Road. "Santa Cruz was a sleeper," Ow notes with a growing smile on his face. "In the wintertime, after 8 o'clock, you could shoot a cannon down the main street and you wouldn't hit anybody. But I read where the University of California was coming in, so I anticipated the growth that was coming. The students and faculty were bound to liven up the economy. So even though 41st Avenue was just a bunch of farm land back then, I was confident of its potential. The property was a dream come true."

Ow named the family's new 25,000 square foot store "King's Market," after he traveled to the Bay Area one afternoon and saw the name on another business. "It looked very majestic, and at the same time, it only had a few letters, so it was cheaper to make the signs, and it was easy to pronounce. And so we were known as 'King's Market.'"

Employing his first-intersection-off-a-freeway theory a few years later, Ow purchased 34 acres in Scotts Valley on Mt. Hermon Road. Ow's brother-in-law, Jun Lee, who later served as mayor of Scotts Valley, arranged the sale of the former Dettling Dairy Farm, and the Ows built King's Foods there in 1966 and developed the area's first large shopping center. Once again, Ow foresaw the tremendous growth that was to hit the area, and his business ventures flourished.

All the while, the Ows' son, George, Jr., was being groomed to take over the family business. Traditional Chinese custom dictated that the eldest son be prepared to handle the rights and privileges of the father, and thus was George, Jr., raised. Ow, Sr., always believed that his eldest child had been born under a lucky star and he developed a confidence in him at an early age.

Ow, Jr., of course, was born in Santa Cruz, and he and his younger brother, David, were raised in the Santa Cruz China-town. His Chinese name was Ow Wing Hong, and the year of his birth, 1943 (the year of the Horse in the Chinese calendar), was the same year in which the Chinese Exclusion Act was repealed. Unlike his ancestors, he would have the full rights of a U.S. citizen. With his parents establishing their grocery business in Monterey in the years following World War II, George remained with his grandmother, Gue She Lee, in Santa Cruz until he was seven years old. It was not an altogether easy time.

Santa Cruz still hadn't fully accepted its Chinese residents by the 1940s, and the Santa Cruz Chinatown remained a community somewhat separate and apart from the rest of the city.

When the six-year-old Ow first attended Laurel School (now the Louden Nelson Community Center), he remembers being "teased and jostled" by his classmates for being Chinese. "It was terrible," he says with a lump in his throat and tears welling in his eyes. "Every day during recess I would be harassed. It was very hard. I'm not sure if the teachers were aware of it, or if they just didn't care, or if they thought the kids were just having fun. It didn't matter. After a while, I just wouldn't go out there anymore. I'd stay in and read. And so I became an avid reader."

The confines of the rickety, wooden Santa Cruz Chinatown thus became a sanctuary for the young Ow. There, he felt safe and secure from the taunts and viciousness of the outside world. He developed a special bond with his hardworking grandmother and with the aging Chinese men who still lived in the Tong house overlooking the San Lorenzo River. "They were very old then; many of them had been born in the 1860s," he recalls. "And, of course, the laws at the time prevented them from marrying. So the kids in Chinatown—and I was one of the first—were kind of like their family. They were always warm and friendly and seemed to enjoy us kids a lot... China-town was actually a great place to grow up. There was the river and the fields and the fruit trees, and we played all over. It was really nice down there."

In the fall of 1950, however, Ow and his brother David joined his parents permanently in Monterey. While he missed the friendly confines of Bellevue Place, he was relieved to discover a more liberal racial atmosphere on the Monterey Peninsula. "It just felt more relaxed. There were a lot of different types of people—Italians, Mexicans, Chinese, Japanese, Slavs, recent migrants from Texas and Oklahoma. It was more tolerant."

But not perfect, and Ow still received an occasional taunt at school. This time he responded differently. "In Santa Cruz, I didn't have the confidence to fight back. There just seemed to be too many of them. But in Monterey, I didn't feel so alone, and for the first time I fought back. And after that, they didn't bother me anymore."

Ow graduated from Monterey High School in 1960. He was a good student, though not all that academically inspired until he got to Monterey Peninsula College. Still working full time in the family business, he nonetheless graduated summa cum laude in 1963 and was accepted into San Francisco State. From there he graduated cum laude with a B.A. in Business Administration, and in 1966 he earned an M.B.A. at the University of California at Los Angeles.

Two years later, Ow received an education of a different sort, this time in the jungles of Vietnam, where he served as an officer with the Army's 101st Airborne Division and ran a medical supply station near Hue in the grim months following the Tet Offensive.

It was Ow's first time in Asia, and though racist remarks were commonplace when referring to the enemy ("gooks," "dinks," etc.), Ow felt completely at ease with his fellow soldiers. "I was very much a part of my unit," Ow notes. "In their eyes, I wasn't anything but American. I was very proud to serve my country as an officer. My father had served during World War II, and I felt a continuity there. But just like everyone else in Vietnam, I could hardly wait to get home."

Ironically, Ow's grandfather, Lam Pon, who Ow had never seen and who had never returned to the U.S. after his bitter departure in 1930, had just died earlier in the year at the age of 92, only 600 miles north in the People's Republic of China. It was the closest Ow ever came to him.

Ow returned home to Santa Cruz from the Army in 1970 after achieving the rank of Captain. By then his father had decided it was time to pass on the responsibility of running the family enterprise to his eldest son. He was 27 years old.

"I didn't want to follow the old Chinese style and relinquish the power from my death bed," Ow, Sr., says of his decision. "I had great confidence in my kids. The oldest, Junior, had his Master's degree from U.C.L.A. and had been a Captain in the

Army, so I knew that he was ready. Plus, he had all the experience of working in the stores when he was growing up. Everything's turned out real well."

George, Jr., also felt confident about, and honored by, the decision. "I always knew that I was going to work with my family," he says. "There was never any question. My father always said I was born under a lucky star, and from an early age, he trusted my judgment and respected my intuition. I was closing up the Monterey market and handling the money when I was only 13."

"I have, of course, been very fortunate," he continues. "My father and grandfather provided me with a base on which I've been able to build. Lam Pon established roots and connections for my father, and he in turn acquired a great deal of developable property. Lam Pon passed on his business knowledge to my father, who then passed his on to me. I'm very appreciative of that and feel the responsibility of expanding the business base for my extended family and those who came after me."

After taking over the reins of the family finances, Ow, Jr. quickly expanded the Ows' holdings at both their shopping centers by negotiating long-term leases with the likes of Alpha-Beta, Orchard Supply, Thrifty Drugs, World Savings and UA Theaters—leases which have assured the growth and continued success of the two centers. He also supported several of his younger siblings in establishing businesses of their own, and today he works closely with brothers David and Terry, sister Jeannee, and niece Karen (David's oldest daughter) in overseeing the family's shopping centers. Another younger brother, Richard, runs clothing stores at both locations.

"My mind is always open to new ideas," Ow notes. "I learned from my father that the key to being a good businessman is trusting your own intuition, of being open to possibilities. For me, business is very exciting. Flexibility is the key to success. You have to dance lightly."

Now in her mid-twenties, Karen Ow represents the fourth generation of her family to be engaged in business in the Monterey Bay area. "I like the idea of working with the family," she notes. "You have a sense of knowing that everything you do will directly affect those around you, and therefore there's an added sense of dedication." Her grandfather, George, Sr., still makes his presence felt from time to time, and Karen notes an extra sense of satisfaction when working with him. "I really value his feedback and support, and at the same time, I know he appreciates my accomplishments as well. As for working with my dad, well, we've always been close, and this is just an extension of my upbringing. It's wonderful."

In recent years, her uncle George has expanded the family enterprises to include a variety of business ventures and real estate holdings stretching all the way to Chicago. One of his principal partners has been Larry Chew, who Ow took notice of at a party 10 years ago when Chew waxed ecstatic on the art of making pizza. A short time later, Ow and Chew started "The Pizza Company" at the 41st Avenue shopping center, and the business has presently expanded to three locations. They are also partners (along with other investors) in the Capitola Book Café and in the Ows' most recent venture, the Pontiac Grill, located in downtown Santa Cruz. The Ow family holdings include other businesses and a medical center/office building, which is run by Ow's wife, Gail Michaelis-Ow, combining her expertise as both a registered nurse and a real estate broker.

Lest anyone think otherwise, however, the Ows are hardly all business. With George, Jr., as the driving force, the family has established itself as one of the biggest supporters of the arts, scholarships and community services in the Monterey Bay area. At a time when federal economic policy has cut significantly into public coffers, the Ows have generously contributed to artists, community service programs, and aspiring students in need.

One night in 1979, Ow, Jr. was driving down Mission Street

with his eldest son, William. Near the juncture of King and High Streets he spotted someone painting a whale mural on the side of the building. "I was completely engrossed in business at the time," Ow said, "and here was this young guy painting at night with his headlights pointed at the wall. It was remarkable. It touched me. I could see how great it was to have an artistic vision that you could live for. I thought this must have been what Mozart was like—to be connected with the infinite."

The artist was Daniel Burgevin, and Ow soon commissioned him to complete a mural at his 41st Avenue complex. "It struck me that with just a little money and some wall space, there could be a great work of art. There is so much talent in Santa Cruz that only needs a little support to make it blossom. I see myself as a conduit." Since the first mural seven years ago, Ow has supported a series of dance, drama, film, sculpting and writing projects.

The Capitola Book Café has sponsored numerous readings and book-signings, events which Santa Cruz novelist James D. Houston called "significant contributions to the vitality of the cultural community." He adds, "George has become a real important figure here. He's high-minded, a real vital presence."

Jeanne Wakatsuki Houston, who wrote *Farewell to Manzanar* with her husband, said she feels "empowered" by her friendship with Ow. "George's sense of community and creativity reflects my own notion of Asian sensibilities," she explained. "He has a deep feeling of interdependence, of understanding that his own destiny is linked to those around him. He has a unique way of looking at purpose and of encouraging creativity because his own yin and yang energies are in balance. He's been strongly influenced by the Chinese philosophy handed down by his father: you're only as successful as the rest of your community."

Educational opportunities for the disadvantaged are also a

high priority for the Ows (they often point to a favorite family proverb which states: "Plan for one year, plant grain; plan for 10 years, plant trees; plan for 100 years, educate the people"), and the family currently sponsors fifty scholarships for Third World and re-entry women students attending Cabrillo College. Ow, Jr., also helped finance the education of UCSC literature student Maria Elena Gutierrez, the daughter of farm workers, who was recently awarded an Andrew Mellon Fellowship to attend Stanford University. In June of 1988, George Ow, Jr. was named an Honorary Fellow at Cowell College in recognition of his commitment to education.

George Ow, Sr., has also dedicated a good part of his life to community service. Long active in the Scotts Valley and Mid-County Chapters of the Exchange Club, Ow, Sr. was elected president of the National Exchange Club in 1986, the first Chinese-American so honored. In 1988, both he and his eldest son were named "Man of the Year" by the Santa Cruz Chamber of Commerce.

But the awards and community activities only go so far. George Ow, Jr., now in his mid-40s, is once again focusing his energies on his immediate clan. "Probably my biggest challenge at the present time is to learn more about my family, about being a good husband and father," says Ow, who has three sons—William, Benjamin and Andrew. "My wife, Gail, is my teacher in this respect. She's great with the kids, and I feel I have a lot to learn from her. I feel very lucky to have her as a partner.

"Because of the various laws aimed at the Chinese, the old Chinese men I grew up with were never able to have wives or children. How lucky I am to be blessed with such a large family. Sometimes I think it must have been very lonely for them." He paused, as though saddened by the thought. "Yes, very lonely."

Today, there are 13 grandchildren of George and Emily Ow, all of them living in the Santa Cruz area. "I think that the spirits of Chin Lai and Ah Fook and the other old bachelors are coming back to life again in the new generation," says the man, George Ow, Jr., who sat in their laps as a young boy. "I have a feeling that they are all here with us today, pulling for us. If you look at their oppression as a pushing down of their energies and opportunities, today it's like a volcano exploding. And I can feel them here with us. It's a much better time for them to be living."

—1986

LEE GUE SHE
for Luella Lee Churchill

Into the photograph I stare,
and the beauty is unyielding:
the dark eyes, the gentle lips,
the curving of the cheekbone.
Ten thousand miles you have traveled
for a life of the soil,
a hot stove, the cannery,
and seven children
whose lives will always be blessed
by the journey.
You will make a history
not even you can foresee:

blood is more powerful than the past
love more powerful than the future.
That is the wisdom of the old country.

You will not remember me,
the gypsy boy on the sidewalk
with the fish-scale hands
who followed you up the hill to your garden.
I watched you there among the sunflowers
and the giant squash leaves,
your grey hair shining in the summer sun,
your strong hands still moving quickly
and the lines on your face all leading
home.
When you smiled
a thousand butterflies sang Chinese hymns.
I watched your dark eyes disappear
into your memories.

Gone are the seasons by the river
when the fish gathered in the shallows
and the pears grew fat and sweet for the children.
One hundred years is a snap of the fingers.
Death is a mystery
only to those who cannot wait.

—1987

"1001 STAGNAROS"

ONE OF ROBERT "BIG BOY" Stagnaro's earliest childhood
memories is of a small hole next to his father's fish market on
the Santa Cruz Municipal Wharf. Through it he could see the
sparkling blue and green waters of Monterey Bay and a patch
of weathered wharf pilings covered with mussels, barnacles,
starfish and long clumps of seaweed swaying with the tides.
"My life began at the edge of that hole," says Big Boy, the magic
of the memory lingering in his eyes.

Big Boy was four years old then, and his father had cut out
the hole so that his youngest son could fish through it while
the rest of the family carried out the duties of running a fish
business. "He made sure it was small enough so that I couldn't

fall in," Big Boy remembers, "but it was large enough for me to pull fish up. And believe me, I used to catch a lot of fish through that hole."

A few years later, Big Boy was set loose from his tiny fishing grounds and given free reign of the entire wharf. He would scamper from fishing boat to fishing boat, listening to the old Italian fishermen speak in their native dialects about the day's weather and their catches.

Whenever he got into trouble with one of the fishermen, Big Boy would hurry off to an old Model T truck parked across the street from the wharf's fish houses. Inside was his grandfather, Cottardo Peter Stagnaro I, who had a special fondness for his last grandson, given the name Big Boy at birth because he had weighed only one pound and had nearly died in a pool of blood.

Cottardo I was in his seventies and crippled then, the victim of a boating accident years earlier, but there was still a fierceness to his presence as he watched the final days of his life through the windshield of the fish truck. "I was his pet. Nobody could touch me when I was with him," says Big Boy. "He couldn't walk anymore, but he seemed somehow larger than life. I always knew that as long as I was with him, I was safe. Nobody—and I mean nobody— ever crossed him."

The man nobody ever crossed was born in Riva Trigoso, Italy in 1859. By the time he was 10, he was a veteran seaman on merchant ships sailing along the Mediterranean Coast. By the time he was 15, he had crossed the Atlantic three times. In 1874, while his vessel was unloading cargo on the old Santa Cruz Railroad Wharf, he jumped ship and decided to call Santa Cruz his new home.

The young sailor had four sisters in Riva Trigoso, and in the ensuing decades he traveled back and forth between Italy and America, eventually bringing three of his sisters, their husbands and nearly 60 other families from Riva to the west side banks of Santa Cruz. For over 40 years, "La Barranca," as it was called, hosted a thriving Italian fishing colony—and Cottardo I was the recognized patriarch.

Maria Zolezzi Stagnaro, Cottardo's wife, immigrated to the United States in 1898, bringing along with her an adolescent son, Cottardo II. In 1900, at the family home on Bay Street, she gave birth to another son, Malio, and a waterfront dynasty was born.

In the next half-century, Cottardo I and II, Malio and Cottardo II's children fashioned a mini-wharf empire, the C. Stagnaro Fishing Corporation, which would come to include two restaurants, coffee shops, a dozen fishing vessels, three speed boats, a fish market and a marine fuel station. "There were so many of us," says Big Boy, "we had to expand. We didn't have any choice. During the Depression, our business actually grew because of all the hard work we put into it and all the hungry mouths we had to feed. That's when the family got the nickname the '1001 Stagnaros.'"

"The wharf was always exciting back then," he emphasizes. "I couldn't wait for the school bell to ring so that I could go down there and work. I lived for that every day.

"The amount of fish brought in when I was young was incredible. Tons of salmon, sea bass, rock cod, sole and sable fish. There were 75 to 100 boats unloading their catches on any given day, and as soon as the boats were emptied, the men were back at work mending their nets and baiting their lines."

When it was built in 1914, the east side of the wharf was lined with a series of davits, small hand cranes that hoisted the fishing fleet to the dock whenever rough weather was imminent. The building of the small craft harbor in the 1960s brought about the demise of the davits and their departure changed the wharf forever. "The wharf lost its color then," says Big Boy. "We'll never bring those days back."

Big Boy is not the only Stagnaro nostalgic about the wharf's colorful past. If her younger brother's first memories are of fishing, Gilda Stagnaro's are of truck rides with her Uncle Malio and five-cent ice cream cones. "I remember my father buying us ice cream and of listening to the beautiful Italian language of the fishermen," she reminisces. "It was music to my ears, like a serenade or an aria all the time."

While Big Boy and the rest of her brothers worked daily on the boats and in the fish market, Gilda's initial destiny appeared to be far away from the wharf. She was an honors student in languages at Santa Cruz High and had dreams of serving in the diplomatic corps as a translator. Her first job was with the Chamber of Commerce in 1941, but by the end of World War II she was back working full time at the wharf with the rest of her family.

"I filled in everywhere at first—in the coffee shop, the market, handling fish and game tags," she says smiling. "But after a while, I wound up running the coffee shop. You might say I found my niche."

In 1972 the Stagnaros renovated their Sports Fishers Coffee Shop into a full, 134-seat seafood restaurant—Gilda's—and the lady after whom the restaurant was named found herself putting in 18-hour-and-over days, but never time to marry. "I ran myself pretty hard," she acknowledges in a characteristic understatement, "but the family needed me, so I was there."

In the 1980s, Gilda's restaurant is the last remaining holding of the original C. Stagnaro Corporation. A series of family deaths, the decline of the local fisheries and difficult business conditions all contributed to the family releasing itself from its various enterprises. Only Big Boy, Gilda, and Big Boy's children, Dino (recently brought in as a manager) and Laura, remain working in the family enterprise.

"It gets harder and harder each year to make it," declares Big Boy. "Increase in food and labor costs, insurance and rents have all added to our problems. Plus, with all the new businesses on the wharf, parking isn't adequate out here during peak periods. We don't get the kind of overflow crowds in the restaurant as often as we used to."

According to Gilda, the city-sponsored expansion on the wharf has been a mixed blessing. "I feel we were ready for a facelift, but there was a lack of forethought in respect to business conditions. The increase in the number of businesses—with all their additional employees, never mind their customers—greatly exceeds the increase in parking."

In spite of the business demands placed upon them by the modern era, the Stagnaros still manage to bring a little of the cherished old days into their restaurant. "We don't know everyone like we used to," says Gilda, "but our forte here is still the personal touch.

"You know, this hustle-and-bustle today never stops me from recognizing how fortunate we are to live here in Santa Cruz. I always take time to look out the windows and marvel at the sunsets. I used to want to go out and see the world, but now the world comes to me. Visitors from all over the globe walk in each day, and we always try to make them feel at home."

Indeed, it is a lot like the old days, and even if her spaghetti sauce isn't quite as good as her mother's used to be, her smile is just as warm, and the lines around her and her brother's eyes have such rich stories to tell.

—1985

FIFTY SEASONS ON THE SEA:
Victor Ghio

IT'S 4 A.M. AND NOT even the birds are out. A drizzly shroud of fog blankets the California coast, leaving the nocturnal world chilled, wet and inhospitable. For Santa Cruz fisherman Victor Ghio, a veteran of more than 50 seasons on the sea, this is the hour of his beckoning, his moment of truth.

Victor climbs into the engine room of his cedar-hulled boat, the *Catherina G*, checks the water, then the oil and fuel, slips back out as though he were a third his age, ducks back into his cabin and starts his engine. There is a slow rumble, then a roar as the engine takes, and Victor guides his cluttered boat through the jetties of the small craft harbor into the Monterey Bay.

Fishing, according to Victor, hasn't been all that good lately. "It's been absolutely lousy out here," he says with the bitterness of a man who has been robbed of his livelihood. "I'll be lucky if I catch enough to pay for the fuel."

On the eve of his 70th birthday, Victor Cottardo Ghio is truly the old man of the sea, his face lined by a lifetime of sun and wind and salt sea spray. In spite of his years and nearly a dozen major operations, Victor's sea legs remain solid and sturdy. His leathery hands and sinewy arms are strong and sure. There is a sparkle in his eyes and an Italian devilment to his disposition. His broad smile is full of life. "I don't feel old at all," he says emphatically. "No way."

Victor's heart may be young and alive, but it is also heavy with memories of a time when Santa Cruz and its bay were far different. He is the last of his breed, a living monument to a piece of Santa Cruz history that once was and will never be again.

Victor's grandparents, Stefano and Vittorina Ghio, joined more than 60 other young families from the tiny Italian village of Riva Trigoso—including the Stagnaros, Bregantes, Carniglias, Loeros, Bassanos, Castagnolas, and Oliveris—and settled in Santa Cruz near the turn of the century. Victor was born and raised in Santa Cruz's Little Italy, the "barranca" as it was called, nestled on the west side cliffs, and he went to sea at a young age.

"My grandfather was a fisherman. My father was a fisherman," Victor recalls. "Damn near all the Italians in them days was fishermen. When I was 8 or 9 I'd go fishing with my dad on weekends and in the summer. I always loved being out there with him.

"The bay was loaded back then. We'd catch 40 to 60 dozen crabs a night. We'd get 15 cents a dozen for them. Hell, nobody wanted them—not like today. We couldn't give the damn things away."

Other fish were plentiful as well: flounder, sable fish,

sardines, halibut, albacore, sea bass, salmon and rock cod. "In the Depression, we only got 3 cents a pound for the rock cod," Victor recalls. "When my dad first started fishing, he only got a penny a pound."

During the war years, Monterey Bay yielded record catches of sardines and sable fish. Prices soared, but Victor wasn't around for the bounty. He, like scores of other young Santa Cruz Italians eager to prove their patriotism, had enlisted in the Navy prior to the bombing of Pearl Harbor. He didn't return home to settle down until the end of the Korean War in the early '50s. "After 11 years in the service, I'd had enough. I wanted to get back to fishing."

He promptly commissioned the building of a new boat, a 28-foot Monterey style double-ender named after his mother.

"In the winter months, I fished black cod (sable fish) with my brother Lily. We used the old Portuguese long lines—with the baskets—in 200 to 600 fathoms of water. We'd bait anywhere from 3,000 to 4,000 hooks a day.

"Oh Christ, that was hard work. Long hours. When Lily died, that was the end of the black cod fishing for me—there was no one to replace him. You just couldn't find anyone with that kind of experience."

In spring and summer, Victor fished for salmon with old-fashioned "hand lines"—lines literally pulled in by the hands. "I'm telling you, our hands were blistered and calloused so bad that we couldn't even open them up at the end of the day. 500 to 600 pounds of salmon, day in and day out is a lot of fish."

Although not as visible to the general public, changes in the American fishing industry have paralleled those in American agriculture. Big is in, small is out. Just as the last quarter-century has witnessed the end of the family farm and the rise of agri-giants, so, too, has it seen the demise of the solitary fisherman setting out daily to secure his catch.

"If I had to name one thing which has done us in," Victor says with no small amount of fury, "it's those damn drag boats. They've ruined everything."

95

Unlike Victor, who still uses baited hooks to catch his fish, drag boats (the maritime equivalent to mechanical tomato harvesters) use huge nets held down by weights scraping the bottom of the ocean like an underwater bulldozer to secure their catches.

"You can't destroy the bottom life and expect there to be any fish," Victor declares angrily. "The bottom feeds the rest of the sea. With draggers, the scraping of the marine growth goes on 24 hours a day. They wipe out the small fish and the spawners—everything."

Victor believes that the Fish and Game Department should outlaw drag boats and allow only hook-and-line anglers like himself. Not only would it prevent the destruction of the ocean floor, but only those fish large enough to feed on bait would be caught.

The consumer would also benefit, Ghio notes. "Drag-boat fish has been on board three or four days before it's brought in, and it gets smashed in the nets. Hook-and-line fish is brought in daily and unsmashed. Just compare my fish with a dragger's—you'd never want to eat drag-boat fish again."

Drag boats have not been Victor's only problems. Beginning in 1985, Victor hooked up in a fiery "Catch 22" battle with the state bureaucracy over his right to use gill and trammel nets in local waters. It is a traditional fishing practice he had employed for over 50 years. In 1984, partly in response to the growing influx of Vietnamese fishermen out of Moss Landing, the California Legislature passed Assembly Bill 307, which restricted the use of gill and trammel gear to those who had been issued permits as of that year. It also forbade the issuance of such permits to any new applicants until 1990. Those who didn't use their permits in any given season would not be allowed to renew them in subsequent years.

At that time, Victor, then in his late 60s, suffered through an assortment of health problems and did not apply for a license that season. When he went to re-apply for his 1985-86 permit, he was refused one—even though he had never been notified by the state of the new legislation. In essence, Victor was being told that he could no longer make a living as he had for decades because of a technicality.

After wrangling unsuccessfully on his own with the Department of Fish and Game, Victor finally sought help from State Senator Henry Mello. In June of 1986, Mello addressed a letter to Fish and Game Director Jack Parnell, asking him to investigate Ghio's dilemma.

Parnell's assistant, Robert Fletcher, acknowledged Victor's "Catch 22" situation, but said there was nothing his department could do to remedy the problem. "Unfortunately," Fletcher's letter contended, "Ghio did not renew his permit for the 1983-84 season."

Victor, however, did renew his permit that season—the same year the legislation was passed—but not the following year, when he should have been notified of the new regulatory contingencies. In spite of this obvious error, Victor was still not issued a permit, nor was he allowed to appeal his decision.

Victor and Mello did not give up. The State Senator's final solution to Victor's bureaucratic nightmare was to draft legislation which would exempt from the 1984 law those fishermen, like Ghio, who had been denied permits due to illness or injury. Mello's Senate Bill 1471 became law early in the summer of 1988, and on August 28, Victor was allowed to apply for a 1987-88 permit.

Five days later, Victor's application was approved by the Fish and Game Commission, but his victory was tarnished by the tone of the Commission's notification letter to him. "You should be advised," it warned him, "that any future failure on your part to comply with laws and regulations concerning use of that permit will be dealt with in the most severe manner available to the Commission."

The harshness of that statement left Victor both angry and baffled. "I know of nothing that I have done in my fifty years as a fisherman that deserves the threat in the Commission's letter," Victor declared. "If it weren't for Henry [Mello] my nets would still be collecting dust."

For all the elements battling against him, Victor doesn't have any plans to retire from the sea. "If I ever give it up," he says with a wink, "they'd be planting daisies over me."

"Out there," he says, pointing toward the bay, "you're away from it all. You got the fresh air, no people, no traffic. Christ, the traffic's gotten so bad in town that sometimes it takes me an hour to get from the harbor to the wharf with my fish. I love being away from all that—you better believe it."

The shoaling of the Santa Cruz small craft harbor often prevents Victor from going fishing during the winter months, a factor he's come to accept, if begrudgingly: "I've got nothing against the harbor, don't get me wrong, but it's never made me any money. Before the harbor came, we kept our boats on davits (hand hoists) at the wharf. We fished all year round for 50 years—even during rough weather.

"I'll tell you one thing—the most color Santa Cruz ever had was on the old wharf. When they took the davits down (in the mid-'60s), that was all she wrote. Them days are long gone."

Whether or not he's fishing, Victor is constantly at work, either on his boat, his fishing gear, or his house. There's never an idle moment during the day. "The good Lord gave me two good hands," he says while mending some nets on a rainy afternoon. "I might as well use them.

"Look, hard work never hurt anybody. All of my people were hard workers. Too many people today don't want to work. It's a shame, a damn shame."

When he was younger, Victor was a hard player, too, though he never got married. "Oh, I had my fun, I just never found the right girl," he says. Rumor has it that in his youth Victor was something of a ladies' man, and to this day there always seems to be some young admirers hanging out with him on his boat. "I guess they like the romantic image of a fisherman," he declares, "but not too many of them would be willing to put up with the hours."

Since his mother died in the mid-1960s, Victor has lived alone in his Bay Street home, a few blocks from where he was born over 70 summers ago.

He still loves to entertain his many friends and family. He is an artist in the kitchen, especially with fish dishes like Italian *cioppino*.

When someone suggested during the middle of a gourmet meal that maybe Victor should give up fishing and open a restaurant, he laughed and poured another glass of red wine. "You know, I actually thought about that once. I love people and I love to cook." Then his face tightens. "But a restaurant would be damned near like jail. I just have to be out there on the ocean, fish or no fish. Out there you're a free man."

—1986

The Italian Cemetery: Summer
for Kenneth Michael Lamb

I did just as you said, cousin.
The grey graveyard, a faceless runner,
alley dogs, fog
and no way home.
I came to see the old man, but
his nets were to sea.
He never lived on a hill. He was not

born here. The wild one,
lost to a Chinatown lover beneath the streets,
his lantern
burned too long burned out too soon.
That is not the way.
Seven ships for the homeland
leave without him.

The little fish butcher cramped
smaller than a fish box is buried

with his knife, his stone. He died
for the first time they say,
and then again each day. Let's toast
to fish blood on the table, a song,
a final climb to the Tea Cup. I don't think
you're funny like that anymore.

An old Indian woman in the corner
is forgotten. No, cousin, that is not
the way. I would trade all poetry
for another beer with grandmother,
garlic drying in the cellar,
beans in sacks, whiskers
from the lonely one. The names of dead
fishermen are not etched in salt.

The stone of the young one is cracked.
Thieves have chipped away her picture,
the beautiful one,
she was blonde, wasn't she?
So is mine.

On another morning

I am beginning to look forward
to his funeral. We will all be
together, we will ride in long
black cars. Billy and I have
a secret. I will show you where
I am sitting. Grief might be
a passion, but sorrow is another thing.

There were no carnations, cousin,
no tears in the white marble Madonna eyes,
the fallen crucifix,
a broken beer bottle,
two daisies.

Our mothers sleep alone
at night.

—1984

ROOM AT THE TOP:
Don Yee's Tea Cup

IT'S 10:30 ON A THURSDAY night, and already the dark angel on my shoulder is starting to sing sad songs. Nothing that a few Kamikazes can't cure. I roll up the faded green stairs to the Tea Cup Bar and Restaurant on Pacific Avenue, and already Angelito has changed his tune. The smoke is blue and the ambience is Felliniesque, with a dash of Hammett thrown in for kicks. Make it a double.

At the bar, José McCuen has already given up on the bartender and is casting flirtatious remarks at the woman next to him, an anthropology major at the University. He tries his I-spent-the-year-in-Japan line on her, then a stale Gary Hart joke, but she's not biting. The white Buddha on the cash register smiles: he's seen it all before.

A few seats down, Octavio Schwartz is discussing relationships with one of his old girlfriends. His eyes are distant and sincere, as though he were auditioning for a Bergman film. He keeps uttering the words "visceral" and "commitment," trying to score some sympathy points with the Ex. "You're in the wrong flick, Jake," she says. "This is *Chinatown*."

Over in the corner some *City on a Hill* has-beens are drinking Budweiser from the bottle and bad-rapping the local weekly newspapers. Their eyelids are heavy, getting heavier, and there's only one way for them to go. No one ever said it was going to be easy.

On the couches, a loud, self-assured contingent of *City on a Hill* wanna-be's are drinking imports from glasses and bad-rapping both the local weeklies and the has-beens in the corner. Little do they know how hard that road can be.

I find my way to the red velvet sofa where the Mad Photographer and the Mad Farmer are seated with the Tea Cup's proprietor and spirit incarnate, Don Yee. They are talking business.

Yee, as usual, is attired in his customary suit and bow tie. With his jet black hair slicked back perfectly and his casual, yet precise demeanor, Yee is the epitome of dashing. He has overseen these haunts now for over 40 years, back to the days when Santa Cruz was a sleepy and sometimes sleazy backwater town. Indeed, Yee is a living monument to the once thriving nineteenth-century Chinatown, which was located directly across the street from where the Tea Cup now stands. Sometimes, after a few too many Kamikazes, you can see it there—the laundries and opium dens, the markets and barbershops—through the neon reflections in the window.

The earth has circled around the sun many times since Don Yee's birth in Canton, China, just two years following the demise of the Manchu Dynasty in 1912. He was raised in Canton's wild waterfront district—then the West's open door to the Orient—and it was there that he heard stories about the

United States and the opportunities of "the golden mountain."

At the age of 17, unsettled by the impending Sino-Japanese War, Yee decided to make the journey across the Pacific to America. Like many other young Chinese men of his generation, he had numerous family members operating laundries and restaurants throughout the states, and he finally decided upon Pittsburgh, Pennsylvania, as his place of destination. It was the middle of the Depression, and Franklin Roosevelt had just been elected President.

"I didn't speak a word of English," Yee recalls of his arrival in 1933, "but I went to school and studied very hard."

Yee also got his first lessons in the restaurant trade. "My uncle had a Chinese eatery in Pittsburgh," Yee notes. "I learned English in school, but I learned business from bus boys, bar boys and janitors at night."

Yee returned to China in 1939, but with his homeland economically depressed and still at war, he decided in 1941 to return permanently to the United States. Before leaving China, however, he married Lillian, to whom he's now been married for nearly 50 years.

Immigration and financial restrictions prohibited Lillian from coming to the United States at the time, so Yee departed for San Francisco alone. He immediately got a job working in the naval shipyard, then landed a second job tending bar at "The Forbidden City," the legendary Chinese nightclub on Sutter Street. "Best floor show in all of San Francisco," Yee says. "Lots of Chinese show girls."

While in San Francisco, Yee was a member of the Hip Sing Tong, one of the city's fabled Chinese Six companies. "I began to have too much nightlife," Yee says smiling, "so I decided to change my surroundings." A few months after the war ended, he left San Francisco for Santa Cruz.

According to Yee, it was money from a Chinese gambling syndicate that funded the opening of the Tea Cup in the early 1930s, originally located where the Pearl Alley Bistro operates today. Says Yee, "My older cousin, Dan Yee, was the link between the syndicate and the town's business establishment. He ran the restaurant and the bar until the war, when he got drafted into Army Intelligence as a translator. When the war was over, he re-opened the Tea Cup on Pacific Avenue in May of 1946. Right here. Used to be offices of attorney Donald Younger. I came down to join him."

Seven years later, the elder cousin ran into personal and financial difficulties. Don and Lillian, who rejoined her husband in Santa Cruz in 1948, took over the business. By then, the younger Yee had developed a reputation as a straightforward businessman, and local creditors were willing to trust him.

"We almost starved ourselves, but we made it," Yee declares. "Not easy. We worked at least 13 hours a day, seven days a week."

The Tea Cup reached a height of popularity during the late 1950s and early '60s, when local and national dignitaries dined there regularly, including governors and movie stars. Just about anyone who was around back then remembers it as the town's liveliest night spot. In the 1980s, it is once again one of the town's favorite watering holes.

As I sink into my second Kamikaze and stare at the clay statue of the god Kwan'l above my head, Yee explains to me the secret to his success. "You work hard and you just do your best, whatever you do," he says. "Our Chinese philosophy is that way. My grandfather taught me to always be humble and never to disagree with the customer."

"We try to make our lounge the most comfortable meeting spot in town," says Yee proudly. "We keep our bar prices down so that young people can afford to drink here. I think now we have the longest stay of any one business in the county—42 years. I'm already serving the second and third generation of our original patrons." Yee chuckles at the thought. "I always tell my customers, 'You don't have to be thirsty or hungry to come up here. Just drop by and make yourself at home.'"

At the bar, José and Octavio look neither thirsty nor hungry. Beaten is more like it. Call them a cab, Joanie, the party's over. I turn to ask Don why he keeps going.

"Most of my help in the kitchen is from the old country—Hong Kong," he answers in a contemplative tone. "I'm their sponsor. I'm trying to bring them up the way that I was brought up—that's why I keep the place going, to pass that on. I also want to show my appreciation for the patronage of our friends both here in Santa Cruz and all over the world. I want them to know that they have a nice place to come and get dinner or a drink."

The white Buddha on the cash register still smiles.

—1987

PAPER ANGEL:
The Tin Cans and Heavenly Kites of Charlie Lee

CHARLIE LEE LOVES THINGS THAT FLY—birds, planes, bees, butterflies, and especially kites, for they are his link to the heavens.

It is a cold, quiet March morning and the first hint of the new day's light is softly kissing the city. From the dark shadows of lower Laurel Street, Charlie emerges behind the clickity-clack of his ever-present shopping cart, smiling broadly.

Charlie is a familiar, if somewhat mysterious, figure in downtown Santa Cruz, his warm smile and friendly spirit a daily reminder of all that is rich and wonderful and worth saving in our community. He is the spirit of Santa Cruz past, present and future wrapped into one.

As he nears Cedar Street, Charlie stops suddenly and points his finger upward at the white, translucent trail of a jet liner in the eastern skies. "Look, lookie!" he says excitedly in an English that still bears a strong trace of his native Cantonese dialect. "Long tail! Look'a that."

For nearly a minute, Charlie is motionless as he watches with wonder and satisfaction as the plane disappears over the Santa Lucias to the south. His smile broadens. "Way up there," he chuckles, shaking his head from side to side. "Way gone."

Charlie resumes his ritual journey down the street. His attention now focuses on discarded aluminum cans, bottles, wire and stray shopping carts. Sometimes he can be seen behind a half-dozen of the latter, which he returns to various supermarkets and drug stores in the city. Some pay Charlie a small fee for the service, and some do not. "I take them all back to their homes," Charlie says.

At a time when no one seems to save anything, Charlie is a Zen master of recycling, a counterforce to our consumer society and its perpetual wastes. "Lotsa cans this morning," Charlie notes happily. "Musta been big party last night."

And then Charlie disappears again down the quiet streets of the still sleeping city. He has his work to do. Later on when the afternoon winds pick up over the bay and make for perfect kite weather, Charlie will have his own personal date with the heavens.

Born in the Canton region of China nearly eight decades ago, Charlie grew up in a small, impoverished village where a handful of the older men had once lived and worked in America, and Charlie harbored dreams of making the journey across the Pacific.

By the time Charlie was in his early 20s, China was in turmoil over the impending war with Japan, and those who were able sought to escape.

Like many of his other countrymen, Lee sought refuge in the U.S. by claiming that his father had worked here during the late 1800s. "I tell 'em I longtime Californ'," Charlie says. "Now I longtime San'a Cruz." Charlie also had a sister living here married to the grocer Lam Sing, who offered his brother-in-law a job at the Canton Market upon his arrival.

One of Charlie's co-workers at the market in the 1930s was George Ow, Sr., also newly arrived from China. "Charlie was always a very hard worker," Ow remembers. "Very dutiful. Day in and day out, he was always there." Apparently Charlie was also well known for his feats of strength. "He was the strongest of the Chinese in Santa Cruz," Ow continues. "Very broad and sturdy. He used to lift 100 pound sacks like they were nothing. Very strong."

After the war, Charlie saved up enough money to open a restaurant. Charlie's Chow Mein House on Soquel Avenue, which writer Lee Quarnstrom recalls, served dinners during the mid- 1960s for 35¢ a meal. Business was steady, if not all that lucrative, and Charlie was able to put a little away for retirement.

There is an old Chinese proverb that states, "Things are not always as they appear. On the surface of the lake is the reflection, but that is not all there is to the lake." Charlie's life is something like that, quiet on the surface perhaps, but full of mysteries and surprises beneath it, and a dense, inviolable darkness if you probe too deeply. As a so-called paper angel, Charlie has had to live a good deal of his life in secrecy. "Hush, hush," he smiles when the questions get a little too close for comfort. "I tell you later." Only later never seems to come.

Once, many years ago before I had reached my teens, I was riding my bike down Laurel Hill when I spied Charlie in the athletic field at Santa Cruz High. He was flying three kites at the same time, odd looking kites, certainly different than any I had ever seen before. One was in his hand, the other two tied to a fence. I watched in amazement as he tugged at their strings, heartily calling out to them in a language I could not understand. I have never forgotten that moment.

Twenty years later it is nearing noon and a stiff, northwest wind is whipping the flags on the Cocoanut Grove Ballroom and Boardwalk. Charlie is at the base of the Municipal Wharf with a pair of kites, one a 30-foot dragon model from San Francisco, and the other, a beautiful twin-tailed butterfly kite which Charlie himself has made and decorated.

Many people are familiar with the colorful hand-drawn cards that Charlie distributes for Chinese New Year bearing the inscription *"Gung hay fat choy."* His kites are a mobile extension of that holiday art form, delicate, yet seemingly indestructible.

Historians believe that the first kites ever flown were made in China over 2,000 years ago, their original purpose being to carry messages to ancestors residing in the heavens. A variety of designs were developed, all with their own meanings, and later on a "Kites Day" was celebrated on the ninth day of the ninth month, with citizens young and old throughout the country participating in the annual festival. Two millennia later on the other side of the Pacific, Charlie Lee is carrying out that tradition.

Charlie's butterfly kites are made of bamboo and rice paper, which he carefully shapes over a three or four-day period. When the basic structure is completed, he attaches 12-foot tails to the kite and then adds his decorations, which include the Chinese symbols for "happy" and "fly high." If the kite is not perfectly balanced, he adds weight to either side of the structure by wrapping small amounts of string to the bamboo frame. "I learn first in China," he says, "but better here in America."

With the wind to his back, Charlie lifts the kite above his head and waits until the strong northwesterly pulls firmly on the bridle string. He lets go, inching it out slowly at first, and then faster, until the butterfly is a small white dot above the city.

Charlie is ecstatic. "Oh boy!" he shouts. "Beautiful, beautiful. Fly higher than the birds. Butterfly is number one!"

Charlie treats his kites as though they have lives of their own, ascribing to them human qualities. When the wind subsides a bit, then shifts directions, and the kite skitters across the sky, Charlie declares, "He [the kite] no like that. He get angry." Moments later, when the kite settles into its normal flight pattern, Charlie says, "He calm down. Now he happy again."

Charlie repeats the same takeoff process with the dragon kite, and soon there are two dots, one red and one white, drifting over the horizon. A flock of gulls and then a plane cross visual paths with Charlie's crafts, and he points happily to it all, proud that he, too, has his own place in the heavens. "Me and them like cousins," he declares, his eyes fixed on the sky.

After a half-century of living in Santa Cruz, Charlie has lots of friends in town and a few of them stop to chat on their way to the wharf. He greets them warmly and offers them the opportunity to hold the string. There is something entirely relaxing and therapeutic about feeling the power of the wind at your fingertips and sensing that you are intrinsically connected to the object soaring a quarter-mile above you. Perhaps this is one of the many secrets behind the youthful sparkle in Charlie's eyes.

More strollers, this time strangers, pass by and Charlie offers them a moment at the helm. Some take up the offer, and a childhood glee rushes to their faces. Others, however, ignore this aging gentleman with a long life's journey etched into his face, continuing smugly on their travels into the American vacuum, as if they are somehow above it all.

But as Charlie stands there at the base of the wharf, his eyes smiling at the butterfly and dragon dancing in the heavens, one senses it is he who is above it all, his soul and the spirits of 2,000 years rising above the mundane inanities of the earth. There is something in Charlie's kites and cans and shopping carts which we all need to consider and understand.

After a few hours and many exaltations, Charlie decides it is time to bring the kites down from the heavens. He quickly pulls them in, carefully and rhythmically wrapping the strings in perfect patterns. He places everything in the basket of his cart, picks up a can from the beach, and proceeds quietly on his way.*

—1988

* *Bing Ngeow "Charlie" Lee died while working at his home on May 11, 1988.*

HELEN WESTON:
Amazing Grace

IT'S AN EARLY AFTERNOON A few weeks before Thanksgiving, and the November sun shines brightly, if not all that warmly, on the streets of Santa Cruz. In the shadows of the old ice house and the abandoned packing sheds at the juncture of Chestnut and Laurel Streets, a smiling, laughing Helen Weston is in her "realm," as she calls it, distributing food to the poor and hungry of the town. It is the monthly Helen Weston-NAACP fish give-away, and Weston is in a constant flow of motion and conversation as she hands out packages of rock cod, red snapper, sole, and a bit of salmon from the back of a pickup truck she has borrowed from a friend.

"After as many years as I've been involved in this business," says Weston in her charming, high-pitched voice that still bears a strong trace of her southern roots, "you can tell the needy from the greedy. I make sure that only the poor folk get handouts. And don't let nobody here fool you—there be plenty of poor folk in Santa Cruz."

Weston, under the auspices of the local NAACP chapter, has been coordinating the fish distribution for a number of years. She secured the monthly contribution of fish from a local seafood merchant, then developed a phone list of needy community members whom she calls to notify of the dispersals. "As many as 75 families get fish from us each month," she says proudly. "Sometimes we give away over 500 pounds."

On this particularly cool November afternoon, there are packages remaining in the back of the truck and no more takers in the parking lot. It has grown dark, and Weston might well call it a day, but she declines. Instead, she decides to take the fish to the people. "We'll be going into a few low-income neighborhoods," she declares joyfully to her volunteer crew and ushers them into the pickup. "Lot of people there can use this food. Let's get a move on."

Helen Weston has lived in Santa Cruz for over a quarter of a century, and ever since she first arrived here, she has given fully of her time and energy to community service activities. She has held every position, save for president, of the Santa Cruz County NAACP, and continues to serve on various committees of that organization; she is an active member of the Seventh Day Adventist Church, for which she has taught sabbath school and continues to work once a week at its community service center on Cayuga Street; and she served for over five years on the county's Democratic Central Committee, on which she earned a reputation as someone not afraid to do the dirty work.

"Any time there's a task to be done in this town," says longtime community activist Bob Lissner, "Helen does it, no questions asked. She's a tireless worker, and she doesn't seek out a

114

lot of excessive praise like a lot of other people."

"Personally, Helen's one of the most generous people I've ever met," Lissner continued, "always willing to do someone a favor. She's a great friend of this community. I wish there were a hundred more Helen Westons around. Santa Cruz is fortunate to have her."

Indeed, had Weston acted on her first impressions of Santa Cruz, the city might have had her for only a week.

Born and raised in Hope, Arkansas, during the Depression, Weston took her first job as a young girl working as a maid in a rooming house. "My, those were hard days," she remembers. "My mama would wake me up while it was still dark outside. I'd start up work early in the morning, get a couple of rooms cleaned up, then head off to school. Soon as school's over, I'd come on back to the roomin' house, finish up, and then go straight to bed. Next day I'd do it all over again. Wasn't all that easy."

As she grew older, Weston took on jobs as a cook, and later as a doctor's assistant. In the early 1960s, widowed and the mother of a seven-year-old son, Homer, Weston decided it was time to leave Arkansas and move west to California where her sister Alma had recently resettled in a little town called Santa Cruz.

"The day I got here I almost turned around and went right back home," Weston chuckles. "The place looked like country, real country, I tell you. Everything was all torn up downtown, all around, everywhere you go. It was a holy mess. It sure didn't look like any place I wanted to live. I just wanted to be reborn and go on back to Hope."

Her young son, however, took a liking to the place and urged her to give things a try. "It took a while," she grins, "but the town kind of grew on me." She found work as a cook in a local sanitarium and moved into a small but comfortable home on Wilkes Circle.

One thing Weston and her family had to get used to in Santa Cruz was a different feel to race relations. "I know this surprises a lot of people when I say it," she declared, "but I never did have too many problems with white folks in the South. I think people there were used to dealing with each other. There wasn't a whole lot of meddling going on. When I was a little girl, we didn't think nothing about having dinner with a white family. Out here it was different. I tell you, I've met a lot more racial prejudice in California—in Santa Cruz— than I ever did in Hope, or anywhere else in the South for that matter."

While Weston had first joined the NAACP in Arkansas, once she had found her bearings in Santa Cruz, she decided to become an active member of the local chapter. "It was a way of getting to know the rest of the black community," she explains, "and I also wanted to be sure that my family's rights were going to be protected. That's one of the things we were learning about in the '60s."

The Santa Cruz County NAACP, a local chapter of the national organization founded by W.E.B. DuBois in 1910, was quietly formed here in 1948 by a small handful of the black community. By the mid-60s, when Helen Weston joined it, the organization was extremely active and engaged. Although pre-university Santa Cruz wasn't exactly a hot bed of civil rights activity, the energy and consciousness of the national movement gradually had an impact on the sleepy coastal burg. In 1967, at the urging of NAACP Chapter President Sy Rockins, a conservative Santa Cruz City Council declared the last week of January "Negro History Week," and Rockins also demanded that local officials support legislation to protect civil rights workers in the South.

By the 1970s, NAACP members pushed vigorously for a memorial to honor Louden Nelson, the ex-slave, and in 1979 petitioned the city council to rename the community center on Laurel Street in his honor. (Councilmember Joe Ghio cast the lone vote against changing the name.)

Weston was at the forefront of all these efforts and directed

116

other NAACP-sponsored projects as well. Foremost among them was organizing the first NAACP Food Bank in the late 1970s. "Chapter president Jimmy Griffin was looking for someone to distribute food which had been donated to the organization," Weston says, "and I was his 'victim'."

Using the city parking lot between Cedar and Center Streets as her initial base of operation, Weston quickly developed one of the most successful community service programs in the history of the county. And it was all volunteer. The Food Bank's hardy bags of food became weekly staples for a wide cross-section of the city's low-income community.

"I had lots of fun doing the Food Bank," says Weston. "I met and worked with a lot of great people. It was very uplifting. Sometimes I'll be walking down the street and people will come up to me and thank me for handing them out those bags of groceries."

"The basic goal of the NAACP is to help the people," says Weston. "There's just no other way to put it. That's what the Food Bank was all about. We also work to prevent job and housing discrimination—or any other kind of racial discrimination. That's our job."

Weston is miffed by the oft-repeated misconception that "there aren't any black people in Santa Cruz." "I hear that all the time," she says somewhat bitterly, "and I just don't understand it. I know where they are. There be plenty of them around, though they're not always hanging out like a flag on a flag pole. That's not their way."

As chair of the NAACP's membership committee, Weston is continually trying to get members of the black community to join her organization. She also works regularly on both the NAACP's annual Labor Day Picnic at DeLaveaga Park and the Martin Luther King Mid-Winter Festival. And then there are always her monthly fish give-aways.

"Without Helen," stresses NAACP official Luther Wallace, "there wouldn't be a Santa Cruz NAACP as we know it today.

She is an absolute stalwart of the organization. She is relentless in her pursuit of justice. And she is a joy to work with."

For as much time as Weston puts into her NAACP activities, one might expect that to be the extent of her community service work. Far from it. In 1968, during the emotionally charged months of Robert F. Kennedy's campaign for president, Weston got bit by the politics bug, and she has been an active supporter of Democratic Party candidates ever since. "I liked Bobby because he fought for what he knew was right," she explains, the pain of his assassination still written on her face. "He was a friend of black people and I was all for him."

The list of local, state and national politicos Weston has worked for since is a long one: George McGovern, Alan Cranston, Julian Camacho, Jerry Brown, Leon Panetta, Teddy Kennedy, Walter Mondale, Geraldine Ferraro, and most recently, Jesse Jackson.

The highlight of her party service, however, came when she was overwhelmingly elected at a countywide caucus to serve as a Kennedy delegate to the 1980 Democratic Convention in New York City. She was disappointed, though not surprised, by Kennedy's defeat to Jimmy Carter, but is quick to point out the many progressive positions she helped vote onto the national platform.

All in all it was a memorable experience. "It was my first trip ever to New York," she says. "It was exciting, the bright lights and all, and the convention was tremendously educational. When it was over, though, I was happy to get on home. New York was fun, but I wouldn't want to live there. No way."

One gets the feeling that Helen Weston has fun wherever she goes, and on a joyous Christmas Eve, amid the hectic, last-minute hustle and bustle of the holiday rush, she appeared as the epitome of calmness and hospitality, despite seven pies in her oven, granddaughter and a friend playing in the living room, and no doubt numerous errands to complete. "I'm one of Santa's biggest helpers," she said convincingly. "Can't let him down and can't let nothing get me down. That's just the way I am."

As the sweet smells of her holiday cooking and the sounds of laughing children filled the air, Weston talked about the personal motivations that continually move her to help those less fortunate. "The Lord put me on earth to help people," she said, "and that's all the reason I need. I like to be busy. I like doing things. I like getting other people involved. It's just my bag to do the kind of things I do."

Up until 1985, when poor health slowed her down a bit, Weston was an occasional singer at the Missionary Baptist Church on Woodrow Avenue. Her favorite song, she said, was "Amazing Grace." In a voice full of warmth and compassion, she sang the first verse softly:

> *Amazing Grace, how sweet the sound*
> *That saved a wretch like me.*
> *I once was lost but now I'm found,*
> *Was blind, but now I see.*

"Aren't those words beautiful?" she asked. "That's a song about finding the light of the Lord and coming out of darkness. I like trying to share the light of love with people, the light of giving." She stopped and smiled at her granddaughter. It is a very bright light indeed.

—1987

WHITE DEATH:
Jim Vermeulen's Battle Against Asbestos

JIM VERMEULEN HAS LIVED A typically American life. Born in
Grand Rapids, Michigan, just prior to the Great Depression,
Vermeulen and his Dutch immigrant parents moved west to
California in 1932 when he was five years old.

He spent his childhood roaming about the farm communities of the San Joaquin Valley, his father earning a living as a
ring-man at cattle auctions. "Those really were the good old
days," he recalls fondly. "People genuinely cared about each
other's interests, and no one ever bothered to lock their doors.
There was a real sense of community."

During World War II, Vermeulen was a teenage signalman
on a merchant ship in the South Pacific. The merchant crews
were known as "suicide squads," and Vermeulen returned state-
side with a score of shrapnel wounds on his lower body.

He studied automobile body repair on the GI Bill, becom-
ing, by his own account, "a master metal molder." He har-

bored dreams of retiring at Harrah's Club in Reno, taking care of its world-famous fleet of antique cars.

Marriage and a growing family, however, necessitated a shift to more secure employment, so in 1957 Vermeulen found a job as a production coordinator with Johns-Manville Corporation in Stockton. The J-M plant manufactured pipe out of cement and asbestos, and Vermeulen's duties took him to all corners of the dust-ridden factory.

As a way of earning extra income, Vermeulen regularly worked overtime cleaning up the plant and unloading bails of asbestos from boxcars. Often he would return home covered with dust. "It felt like little glass knives in my eyes and throat," he remembers. "My eyes, especially, took a beating." He worked in the J-M plant until 1966. Little did he know then how those nine years at J-M would change his life.

With his four children safely through adolescence, Vermeulen briefly went back to auto repair, then, relying on his experiences at J-M, turned to a career as an industrial safety consultant. He liked his new work, was well-respected by his colleagues, and was asked to teach courses on industrial safety at Fresno State University. In the mid-1970s, however, he began to slow down. He felt tired a lot and lacked the pizzazz which had always been his trademark.

Though he was only in his forties, Vermeulen had to give up his work. He was having trouble breathing.

Today, like three million other Americans, Jim Vermeulen is dying of asbestosis, a debilitating lung disease caused by the inhalation of asbestos particles. He says with no small amount of bitterness, "I am another murder victim of American industry."

When Vermeulen's disease was discovered by doctors in the spring of 1977, he wasn't sure which way to turn. The depression of losing his job and not being able to support his family overwhelmed him. His workers' compensation claim was successfully challenged by Johns-Manville attorneys, while his application for Medicaid was denied because his disease was occupationally related. He was caught in a Catch-22 of the American public health bureaucracy.

Vermeulen had a dozen grandchildren by then. The thought of not sharing his retirement with them was too much for him to face. One day, he placed a gun to his head and began to squeeze the trigger. "I'm not quite sure why I didn't do it. Something just told me to wait a moment, so I did."

During the next few years, Vermeulen searched out information on asbestos and the disease which it precipitates. He discovered that 27 million American workers had been exposed to asbestos during the course of their careers, many of whom, like he, were slowly dying of asbestosis. Another 650,000 had developed asbestos-related lung cancer, while untold numbers had mesothelioma, a fast-acting cancer which attacks the lining of the lungs and stomach and which is always fatal.

The human tragedy which these figures represented disturbed Vermeulen greatly. He had trouble sleeping at night.

In a matter of months, his frustration and despair turned into anger—his anger into resolution.

In July 1980, shortly after moving to Santa Cruz, Vermeulen founded Asbestos Victims of America (AVA), a nationwide organization dedicated to assisting those suffering from asbestos-caused diseases and to warning the public about the dangers of asbestos. The organization further serves as a support group for victims of what Vermeulen calls "the biggest mass murder in the history of the United States."

"It may be too late for people like me," says Vermeulen. "My lungs are saturated with asbestos fibers and covered with scar tissue. But what about the next generation of workers? I've dedicated my life to making sure it doesn't happen to them."

The long history of asbestos use—and abuse—is both sordid and tragic. Asbestos is a common mineral mined from rock forms which readily separates into long, flexible fibers of microscopic proportions—so small, in fact, that 50,000 of them could fit on a single human hair. Its use as a construction material dates back to antiquity.

The Greeks referred to asbestos as "the magic mineral" because of its fire resistancy, while the Roman historian Pliny recorded the use of asbestos in the construction of baskets and pottery. Pliny also noted that the slaves who worked with the substance frequently developed difficulties in breathing, which hindered their capabilities as workers and later resulted in their deaths. The name which Pliny gave to that condition which we can call asbestosis may have lacked scientific sophistication, but it was simple and to the point: he called it "the death of slaves."

Over 2,000 years later, British factory inspectors were alarmed by similar conditions among asbestos workers in London, most of whom were women. In 1906, Adelaide Anderson, Britain's "Lady Inspector of Factories," issued a report which declared: "Of all injurious dusty particles of which I have received complaints, none surpasses in injuriousness to the workers the sieving, preparing, carding and spinning processes in asbestos manufacture."

In virtually every plant which Anderson visited, there were reports of respiratory illnesses and deaths among employees. She included in her report detailed interviews with many of the victims—but it would be well over a half-century before American workers were informed of such hazards. This omission was no accident.

The leading manufacturer of asbestos products at that time (and for the next 50 years) was the Johns-Manville Corporation. Founded by an enterprising young inventor named Henry Ward Johns, the company produced roofing, plumbing, insulation and other construction materials in its U.S. plants, and operated mines in Canada. Ironically, Henry Johns died in 1898 of a chronic lung disease, now thought to be asbestosis.

In 1918, based on reports of asbestosis in a number of medical journals (mostly British), Prudential Insurance Company declared that it would no longer issue life insurance policies to those who encountered asbestos particles in their workplace. By the 1920s medical researchers had established definite links between asbestos inhalation and lung cancer, and beginning in 1929, lawsuits were filed against Johns-Manville by employees claiming disability from various lung ailments. They received out-of-court settlements, meaning that no legal precedent indicating guilt had been established.

The attorney who handled J-M's legal matters throughout this period was Vandiver Brown. During the course of his corporate legal career, Brown successfully prevented the publication of asbestos hazards in a number of trade and scientific journals. He informed other corporate heads that it was J-M's policy not to tell employees about asbestosis because of the potential financial implications of such disclosures. He also lobbied steadily against government regulation of the asbestos industry.

For nearly two more decades, profits remained more important to J-M than people's lives. It wasn't until 1964, at the prompting of the federal government, that labels began appearing on J-M's products, and as late as 1971 when J-M employees were fully informed about the hazards associated with asbestos.

According to Wilbur Ruff, former manager of a J-M plant in Pittsburg, California, the company deliberately withheld critical information from its employees when company doctors discovered asbestosis or cancer in workers during annual medical examinations. This policy, Ruff declared, continued well into the 1970s. Ruff himself had been informed by company officials in 1940 that asbestos caused lung cancer, a fact which he kept from colleagues for three decades.

"They led us to believe that the stuff was harmless, that you could eat it, play with it, do what you will with it," says Vermeulen. "Never once did they warn us about the dangers. As far as I knew, asbestos was perfectly safe."

Johns-Manville employees were not the only American

workers subjected to lethal doses of asbestos in the Twentieth Century. During World War II, 4.5 million men and women went to work in Naval shipyards, quickly churning out vessels for the American wartime fleet. Next to steel, asbestos was the most common material used in ship construction. "Shipyard workers chopped, hammered or squished asbestos around pipes and boilers for insulation, throwing off a flurry of fibers that looked like someone had playfully scooped up a handful and tossed it into the air like confetti," notes labor historian Larry Reibstein. "Sometimes someone did just that."

While the number of asbestos victims climbed steadily in the 1980s, so, too, did the number of lawsuits against asbestos corporations and their insurance carriers. By 1984, there were well over 25,000, and the suits created both a tangled web of litigation and a judicial nightmare for the victims. Not surprisingly, lawyers—on both sides of the issue—proved to be the only real winners in the legal fiasco.

According to a study conducted by the Rand Corporation, only 4,000 workers have received financial compensation (totaling $236 million) in the last 15 years, while lawyers have received $764 million—over three times that amount. "We are making one segment of society extremely rich," says Vermeulen. "And I am referring to the legal profession."

As a result of mounting legal costs and the prospect of future settlements, Manville Corporation (the company dropped Johns from its name in 1981) filed bankruptcy in 1983 as a way of avoiding legal and financial responsibility for its victims. The "Manville Maneuver," as it was referred to in legal circles, placed a large portion of currently pending asbestos litigation on hold and left future suits uncertain.

The Manville move had two major effects. First, it transferred suits from state and federal courts (in which there is a right to a jury trial and an assessment of punitive damages) to bankruptcy court (where neither right exists). Secondly, after six months, no new claims can be filed against a company that has already declared bankruptcy—so that those who discovered asbestos-related illnesses after February 1983 could no longer sue Manville for damages.

While Manville has been the primary target of asbestos litigation, over 100 other companies have also been named in civil suits. In May 1984, 16 of the largest companies and a dozen insurers agreed to form a fund which would pay asbestos victims directly.

A year later, the most significant legal proceeding in the history of asbestos litigation took place in San Francisco, where California Superior Court Judge Ira Brown presided over a legal circus which lasted well over a year. The trial included seven asbestos producers (including Manville), 75 insurance companies and 96 law firms.

At the beginning of the San Francisco court proceedings, Vermeulen and other asbestos victims carried pickets outside the courtroom. "They've spent $200,000 on the building, an equal amount on computers and millions more on attorney fees," protested Vermeulen. "What have they done for us?"

Leanna Noble, AVA's Bay Area organizer, echoed Vermeulen's sentiments: "While they are spending money having an expensive court fight, not a penny is going to the victims."

Back at AVA headquarters in Soquel, on the other hand, pennies go a long way. The four-room office is almost always ablaze with activity, with Vermeulen usually at the center. He is a combination Santa Claus-Philadelphia lawyer, a man with a heart of gold and a rich sense of humor, yet calculating and fierce when it's time to get down to business. His staff is utterly devoted to him.

Vermeulen's personal desk is tucked away in a dark corner of the AVA's smallest room—no ocean view, no big leather chair. The decor is modest—if not stark—save for a few mementos which Vermeulen has accumulated in his nationwide appeal on behalf of asbestos victims. There are photos and books signed by such luminaries as Studs Terkel ("To Jim...a real American hero"), House Speaker Tip O'Neill ("...you're a great fighter"), and Phil Donahue ("To Jim, who is saving lives...").

But Vermeulen's real treasures are the moving letters he has received from asbestos victims and their families. Some are truly tragic: "I am writing this for my husband," begins a letter from Corning, California. "We thought maybe you could help us, or at least tell us we are not alone and there is a group who cares...We have a work compensation case going for three and a half years and it has been a nightmare, as his company is fighting it. They sent him to a doctor who spent five minutes with him and wrote a 45-page report saying there was nothing wrong. What I'm hoping is that you could tell me where to go next. Time is running out for my husband. All his dignity and self-worth have been taken away."

Another from Glenn Ellyn, Illinois, reads: "I have worked in automotive shops for 31 years. Never once have I seen a notice on a brake-shoe box, warning that the linings are made of asbestos. In 31 years I have handled thousands of brake shoes. I now have only 25 percent lung power. I can't even blow out the candles on my birthday cake."

Those of the survivors are the most heart-rendering: "I lost my dad a year and a half ago. He was a plumber and died of lung cancer, which the doctors said was directly related to asbestos. He was only sixty years old at the time.

"At the end, he couldn't even look at us—it hurt him to know he was dying and wouldn't see us anymore. We were all present when Daddy died. Our life and my Mother's will never be the same again."

Such letters make Vermeulen all the more determined to carry on the fight of AVA. In spite of his health condition, his calendar is filled with speaking engagements across the country. He is constantly lobbying state and federal officials on behalf of his membership and has developed strong links between AVA and labor. One of his biggest enemies these days is the Reagan Administration.

"I sometimes wonder if our President has left the human race," says Vermeulen, pointing to a recent AVA newsletter. "As the AFL-CIO has charged, the Reagan Administration's proposed standard on asbestos has nothing to do with worker protection, but is merely a public relations gimmick."

In the shadow of his AVA office, Vermeulen's face turns hard at the thought of the federal government's inaction concerning the asbestos epidemic. "The asbestos industry knowingly allowed us to work with a killer," he states angrily. "Why? For profit, that's the answer. Now we, the wounded workers, are sick and dying, and nobody gives a damn about us. Murder by American industry can no longer be tolerated."

As Vermeulen speaks, his voice gets rough, then fades slightly. He is forced to take long breaths of oxygen from the bottle he is carrying on his hip. The high pitched banter of young children playing across the street at Soquel Elementary School filters in through his window and mixes in with his breathing and then with his voice as he resumes his speech.

"My lungs are going," he says, his blue eyes wide and open to his soul. "I'm not going to be around forever. Somebody is going to have to take my place. We need help. We need more people. Finances are one thing, but what we need here is energy. There's so much talent in Santa Cruz, people have so much to offer. We need some of that talent here. Who's going to help these people out?" *

—1985

* *In 1987, Vermeulen's health problems forced him to resign from his duties at the AVA.*

HOW READING JIM HOUSTON TAUGHT ME
TO APPRECIATE MY HOME TOWN
IN A LITERARY KIND OF WAY

I'M NOT SURE NOW OF the exact circumstances, though it was
sometime in the early '70s that my cousin Kenny handed me a
book called *Gig* by James D. Houston. I was still in high school
and had not yet taken to reading, and the thought of strug-
gling through a whole novel really wasn't all that appealing.
"The guy who wrote it lives here in town," my cousin said.
"Pretty good book."

It was months before I opened it, but once I did, *Gig* was
hard to put down—or at least relatively hard for someone who
would rather be shoveling horse manure than holding a book
in his hands. I remember being amazed by Houston's opening
lines: "There's a restaurant outside of town, above a bay where

vacationers come to fish in the summer and lie around on beaches. It's a wide bay, protected by a jutting headland. At night the restaurant's orange table candles and ties of colored lights reflect in the water so that it resembles, to boats offshore, a casino on the Riviera. . ."

That was Santa Cruz he was writing about, my hometown, in the pages of a real book. I kept rereading *Gig's* opening chapter, delighting in Houston's rich descriptions of the sights and smells and, most important, the feel of Santa Cruz. Never before had I realized that one could actually write about where one was living. All of the other books I had been forced to read in my youth were about far-away places—Paris, London, New York—but Houston was writing about the here and now, about the soil beneath my feet. This was an important discovery for someone who thought he might one day want to be a writer (never mind the fact that he didn't yet like to read). It gave a new legitimacy and urgency to everything I wrote in senior English.

I read Houston's next novel, *A Native Son of the Golden West,* my first summer out of high school. By then I had begun to read voraciously, trying to make up for lost time in between baseball and farm work, and Houston was now being joined by the likes of Hemingway, Steinbeck, Twain, Salinger, Brautigan and Fitzgerald. In my eyes at least, he compared quite favorably, given that he was still writing about a place and a way of life (in this case surfing) that I could claim for my own. Although it would be years before I would actually meet him, Houston possessed a literary voice that felt close and familiar. It felt like home.

It was to be four years before I read Houston again, this time his nationally acclaimed novel *Continental Drift.* Four years can be a long time, especially when a college career is sandwiched in between, and by then I had lost my hometown naiveté. In 1978 I was an angry young man, steeped in the writings of Marx, Mao and Ché, ready to change the world and to make revolution. *Continental Drift*, focused as it was on the relationships of a middle-class Santa Cruz family, thus seemed tame and provincial to me, not to mention apolitical.

While I remember enjoying various passages of *Continental Drift*, particularly vivid references to the old Catalyst and the Santa Cruz Mountains, I dismissed it at the time for not being socially relevant. I was asked to review it for a now-defunct local weekly and declined.

Five years later I was presented with a similar offer from the San Francisco *Review of Books*, this time for Houston's nonfictional *Californians*. I accepted, and quickly set about writing a harsh, political critique. Once again, I loved certain portions of the book, especially a moving portrait of Houston's father dying of cancer, but I felt that it spent too much time celebrating the comfortable, white-wine and college-educated population of California. Looking back, I now realize that I really wasn't criticizing Houston's book, but rather the book I wanted him to write. We had a bitter exchange in the next issue of the *Review*, neither one of us giving any ground.

Two years later, I still hadn't met the man, though as I was to find out, we lived, at the time, within a mile of each other. Occasionally, our articles would appear simultaneously in local publications, but our physical paths never crossed. In the spring of 1984, however, I became involved in a film project with Houston's eldest daughter, Corinne, and later was asked to write an article about a book which his wife, Jeanne, had written with a Vietnam vet. Santa Cruz is a small town and our roads had finally converged.

We met on the second-story deck of his aging, magnificent East Cliff home, the sun just beginning to break through a damp, early-morning fog. Tall and angular, Houston is built like a Cumberland pine. Part WASP and part mountain man, with a touch of Cherokee thrown in for good measure, he appeared on the deck quietly and gracefully, as is his style. He grasped my hand firmly, nodded hello, and peered into me with his probing brown eyes. He was friendly, if reserved, courteous and good-natured. He never said a word about my review of *Californians,* and probably never will. In all honesty, I was relieved.

Since then, I have read and reread most of his many books: *Gasoline, Farewell to Manzanar*—written with his wife and which chronicles the plight of her Japanese-American family through World War II—and *Love Life,* narrated from the perspective of a young woman who has just discovered her husband is having an affair and which is set during the great storm of 1982. Recently I discovered a little known wonder of his called *Writing from the Inside,* which is full of tidbits and suggestions and anecdotes about writing.

Houston has made me laugh, cry, think and despair. Occasionally, he irks me when our politics still differ. But all the while I marvel at the mastery of his craft, the careful and precise way he places words on a page and shapes his stories.

And then, in the fall of 1987, came *The Men in My Life,* published by Creative Arts Book Company in Berkeley. It is a wonderful and moving collection of essays on what Houston calls "kinship," those inviolable ties which have bound him by blood, duty, art and fate to other men throughout his life.

Perhaps it is because I am currently settling into family and fatherhood, a little less angry than a decade ago, that I am so joyfully appreciating Houston's writing once again. I think it is fair to say that a sense of family and troubled roots rests at the center of all his works, and he is a keen observer of that volatile, complex web of relationships.

Blood is thick, Houston is saying. Life is a long haul. A life of writing is even longer. The pine bends, but it doesn't break.

—1987

AT TWENTY-FOUR

I see the boys of summer in their ruin
Lay the gold tithings barren,
Setting no store by harvest, freeze the soils.
                                        —Dylan Thomas

I

HE PEDALED HIS BIKE TO THE edge of the cliff and slowly climbed down to the beach. The sand was warm, but not hot like it had been in July and August, when the sky and sun shone blue and gold and you knew there was nowhere else in the world you would rather be. It was late October now, and it would be April, maybe even May, before you could immerse yourself in the sand again. Five or six months was a long time.

He walked down to the water and put his feet in. The ocean was much cooler than it had been just a few days before. He looked up at the waves crashing against the point, silver sparkles falling across the horizon. He nodded his head and smiled. It was the first northern swell of the year. A storm in Alaska had sent these waves a thousand miles and more along the Pacific Coast, and they would tug and tear and pull away all winter long at the white sand beaches.

He turned his back on the water and looked up at the perfect little patch of sand nestled between the cliffs and cypresses and willows. He had been coming to the same beach for over ten years, nearly half his life. It had been a playground then, and it still was, only the rules had changed imperceptibly through the years.

Tomorrow would be his twenty-fourth birthday. Nearly a quarter century twisted and spinning somewhere behind him. Time, he thought, was not on his side. He had been voted "most likely to succeed" in high school, but there had been no success. Only a succession of meaningless jobs and a broken marriage. He was still playing kids' games. And he was alone. All his friends were in school or back at work. Some had left town for good. He recognized no familiar faces on the beach, now all but deserted. Eddie and Robert weren't throwing the ball around. Michelle wasn't there smiling. Not even Wags was up in the ice plant drinking beer.

II

The bar was dark and crowded and full of smoke, and they had to wait some time for a table. Finally, they sat down. The two men had already had one beer, then another, when the older of the two suggested that the younger might well consider the offer of a job with this bright, young politician named so-and-so. He went on for a number of minutes. "You know, he may not be very good on the issues, but his father has money and old connections, and he'll probably go a long way. Your time will be well invested."

The young man sat back. He had listened, though not attentively, and his mind had wandered in and out as his friend spoke. He thought for a moment about the image of time investment. It made him uneasy. "We'll see," he said, hoping to dismiss the matter.

Then the conversation turned to the town in which they both now lived, the town in which the younger man had been born and raised. The older man spoke of progress, the "right kind" of progress, mind you, the right kind. On this occasion the young man did not listen to his older friend. Instead, his mind skipped and jumped through the lupine and mustard-weed fields to his mother and the old Italian settlement on the west side cliffs. He thought of his grandmother, too, and of her mother, Celestina. Strong women, they were. Four generations in the same soil, and his mind skipped back and forth, here and there, then and now. There was no escaping the erosion, the generational entropy, the decay. Fire to ashes and ashes to earth.

The older man spoke up. "Another beer?"

"No," the young man answered, and he got up from their table and walked out into the night.

III

It was late, getting on towards midnight, and he approached a house seemingly ablaze with energy, lights on figures darting in and out of autumn grey shadows, silhouettes dancing feverishly across velvet drapes. He drew closer and heard Jimmy Cliff blasting over a sound system, many of the party-goers singing along: *("The harder they come, the harder they fall...")* It was one of his favorite songs. The door opened momentarily. He recognized a few faces, all belonging to students at the university. They were the children of lawyers and doctors, aerospace engineers and corporate executives, and they went about their partying the same way they went about their business, with an air and confidence (an arrogance, really) possessed only by children of their class. *("As sure as the sun will shine, I'm gonna get my share of what's mine...")* This verse was joined in with even more enthusiasm, as if those children of opulence had somehow been denied their due. His stomach tightened. Damn it, that's my song, he thought, not theirs. They already got their share.

A lone woman in a rugby jersey drank beer on the porch steps. Her face was blank, expressionless. He turned to leave and realized that he used to mow the lawn there, kept up the garden for old grandma Wells. Fifteen years ago. For 40 cents a week. The Supremes came on. Oreo Motown. They sang for Nixon when Hanoi burned. *("Baby love, my baby love...")* Another old favorite. Everyone joined in. Diana Ross and Jimmy Cliff and white would-be lawyers from L.A.

IV

Tonight he had learned a lesson. It was a lesson on loneliness, a lesson on pain, of the kind that tears at one's heart. It was his town he would always claim, his little burg, full of family and friends and old flames. But tonight, when the pain was full and deep, when the tears welled up in his eyes and he could not bring those eyes to look up at the sky, he knew of only one salvation, only one sheltered cove in the sea he called home, and that was in the arms of his lover.

How full of irony it was, how nearly comical, that someone with no roots here, with no family, could provide him with his lone sense of place, his own protected psychic womb. He had strolled these streets all his life, and now only a foreigner gave him solace. Sometimes things take a funny turn.

It was getting cold. He shivered slightly and forced himself to look up at the sky. Orion gazed down on him, strong and powerful. He took a deep breath. The fog was beginning to roll in, the salt and seaweed moisture clinging to his face. He walked over to her house. It was late and the lights were out. He knocked on the door. After a moment or two, she came to the door wrapped in a sheet. "I'm sorry," she said, but she didn't have to say anything. He could see the outline of another figure on her bed. "I'm sorry." He felt sick and empty. He tried to turn away, but he couldn't move. There was silence. A shooting star fell far into the darkness. Fire to fire to ice.

—1982

BARFLY

MY FRIEND BECKMAN IS A diehard Bukowski fan. He's read everything from *All the Assholes in the World and Mine* to *Love is a Dog from Hell,* and he went to see the movie *Barfly* six times.

"*Barfly* was a piece of shit," I say to him. I am trying to be combative.

"Whadda ya mean? It was great."

"Come on. It was just some Hollywood pap. The characters were about as deep as a two-ounce shot glass. All the women were either whores or crazy, and the men were either losers or jerks. Stereotypes, that's it."

"Whadda ya expect in a movie about dives?" he retorts defensively, "kings and queens?"

"Don't get me wrong, Beckman. I love Bukowski. But *Barfly* was off. You know that Neil Young song 'Meet the losers in the best bars, meet the winners in the dives'— well Bukowski gets it, we get it, but the movie didn't."

"The movie lacked...understanding," I continue. "About why the people are there. About who they are, and what their lives are all about. About having fun. Come on. Let's go for a ride."

Beckman looks a little nervous. He senses it's going to be a long night.

Paul's Tavern out on Mission Street next to the Tip Top Café is a beacon in the night, or better yet, an oasis, the last— and only—hard liquor bar on Santa Cruz's west side. Established by the late Paul Pappas four decades ago, the bar has withstood the onslaught of sociological change wrought on that side of the city by the coming of the university, and it has slithered into the 1980s bloodied, perhaps, but unbowed.

It is here that Beckman and I begin our existential slalom course through the city, a late-night run of the neighborhood drinking establishments from Santa Cruz to Capitola.

"I'm on the lookout for ghosts," I say to Beckman as I slam down my first tequila and orange. "That's another thing *Barfly* left out. There's ghosts all over the place in these joints."

Beckman nods his head and sips from his 7-Up. He's driving. "It's your night to prove me wrong," he says. "Whatever you want."

Over at the pool table, Luis and Juan from Michoacan in central Mexico are finishing up their game. Willie and Waylon's version of "Dock of the Bay" is blasting on the juke. Luis has just performed a magnificent bank shot on the 8-ball and celebrates with a whoop and a long slug of Budweiser.

Luis is 25 and the father of two children back in Mexico. He speaks little English. He pulls out his wallet and shows me a picture of his wife and kids. "I come up here for the money," he says. "Down there it is very poor." He is short and stocky, with soft hands and a big, broad smile. But the smile only lasts so long. "Sometimes the pain of missing my family is very great. It hurts me right here," he says, holding his chest. The balls are racked, and he is ready to shoot his next game. We say goodbye.

Beckman takes Swift Street down to West Cliff, and the moon shining brilliantly over the bay tonight is spectacular.

"All right," Beckman concedes. "There's no one like Luis in the movie. But that guy at the bar with the dragon tattoo was straight from the flick." We pass by the Dream Inn and roll down Beach Hill.

The Avenue Bar on lower Pacific often plays the forgotten stepchild to its counterpart, the Asti, two doors down, but it has an ambience all its own. The wide, sweeping mural of the Santa Cruz waterfront behind the bar is one of my favorites, and its juke-box is the only one I know of with Nat King Cole's "Mona Lisa." I roll a couple of quarters in and play it five straight times.

It is here where I encounter my first ghost.

A distant relative of mine who shall remain nameless was a regular at the Avenue many years ago. He had been a fish cutter all his life, and everyday after work he'd walk from the wharf down to one of his favorite watering holes and drink his daily pay, which in later years, at least, was always in cash. The next day, he'd do it all over again.

After my second tequila I can feel him here in the bar, his hard arms and his Camel-and-whiskey breath and his pent-up frustrations. Whatever it was that was tangled up inside him, he kept to himself. It is his favorite song that I am playing on the juke.

Do you smile to tempt a lover, Mona Lisa?
Or is this your way to hide a broken heart? . . .

Bill, the bartender, a former cabbie, remembers my relative from the old days. "He was quite a character," he laughs. "A lot of energy."

One of the old-timers at the end of the bar, all whiskers and broken teeth, remembers him too. "That little son-of-a-bitch loved to fight," he says. "Soon as anybody says he smells like fish, he'd jump off his stool, and bam, down that other fellow'd go."

Beckman and I tiptoe past the gelato parlor and duck into the Asti. Once inside, we stare into the glass eyes of the deer with the funny antlers mounted on the wall, along with the bowling trophies and football banners from last year's Super Bowl contestants. This is America.

The bartender, Mark Cattani, and I went to high school together, and he greets me with words that cannot be repeated here. He is a big and burly man with a rough-and-tumble demeanor, but beneath it all is a nice little lover boy who used to shoot rubber bands at old ladies.

"What do I call this kind of place?" I ask him. "Is it a tavern or a workingman's bar or what?"

"I like to call it a neighborhood bar," he says. "Look around you. We got all different types of people in here. Old folks, young folks, workin' stiffs and professionals. We got darts, shuffle board, a good juke. And we never have any trouble in here. Never. People come here to have a good time."

As Cattani takes care of some more patrons, an older woman three or four seats down says to me with a serious look on her face, "It's a dive, honey. Can't ya tell a dive when you see one?"

While Beckman picks up a game of shuffle board, I scoot down to my new acquaintance. Her name is Lucille. The closer you get, the harder the look becomes, and I soon discover why.

Born in Arkansas around the time of World War I, Lucille and her family were wiped out by the Dust Bowl during the Depression, and they suffered through a Grapes-of-Wrath journey to California in 1933. "I got married the first time when I was 16," she tells me. "Then my husband just left me flat out with our baby girl two years later. Just left. Never saw him again."

She found work as a waitress in a bowling alley near Coalinga, where she lasted nearly 20 years while raising her daughter. "Never had a vacation all that time." She moved to Seaside in the '50s, finding work in the mess hall at Fort Ord. She retired in 1974 and moved to Santa Cruz. Hasn't seen her daughter in 15 years. "Drifted away, I guess. Married to a doctor."

I order a second round from Cattani and watch Beckman at the shuffleboard. He's made a group of new friends, and finally, I have to pull him away.

We're both getting a little tired of the downtown and decide to pass on Bei's, which clearly qualifies on the itinerary, and the Poet & Patriot, which doesn't serve hard booze. Gone is the Caravan, a Bukowski-type bar if there ever was one in town; the Catalyst, Santa Cruz Hotel, Blue Lagoon, and the other restaurant bars are all a little uptown for tonight. And the Tea Cup, of course, is in a league all by itself.

That leaves us with one last stop downtown, the Lighthouse Lounge, located next to the card room on Front and Soquel. Most Santa Cruzans, I've discovered, don't even know this place exists. And that's too bad, as it houses one of the best jukes in town and a dark and cozy little dance floor.

Johnnie, from the Yellow Cab Company in San Jose, is drinking coffee, ready to drive over the hill for a graveyard shift. He buys both of us a drink. "Don't see young fellas in here too often," he smiles.

He's been driving cabs for nine years. "Never had a problem yet," he says. "Most drunks are happy to get home." He looks at his watch and says he better "get goin." We're running behind schedule, too.

We drive by the Seaside Tavern (or "The Cavern," as we call it), never my favorite place anyway, and on up to Brady's Yacht Club. Brady's is a Santa Cruz landmark, and an ugly rumor persists that it is going to be torn down for a redevelopment project on lower Seabright.

Although never to be confused with the St. Francis Yacht Club in San Francisco, Brady's is a bright, lively establishment with a salty, if not exactly nautical clientele. The bar hosts an all-but-vanishing pinball machine, a small but adequate pool table, and a thoroughly eclectic juke.

The Lord knows I spent too much of my youth in Brady's when I should have been home reading Joyce, but there is something irresistible about the place. Perhaps it is all the historical knick-knacks that circle the bar, including a photo of my aforementioned fish-cutter relative singing at some waterfront celebration 50 years ago.

Across the room, Beckman spots a woman he went to Santa Cruz High School with in the early '70s. Three kids, two husbands, and a million cigarettes later, she still looks healthy and lively, and Beckman sidles up next to her.

Seated next to my right is an old fisherman friend who doesn't seem to recognize me. Just a few years ago, he used to scream ferocious obscenities my way, when, as a boat painter at the harbor, I played the radio loud enough to hear it in Lompico.

After a few moments, recognition finally sets in. "You ol' sum'bitch," he growls. "How the hell are ya?" Not too bad, I tell him.

"Fishin' has been the shits lately," he says, "and it's gettin' worse. It stinks."

He is drunk and forgetful, I suppose, and he once again asks "How the hell are ya?" Not too bad, I say, better than the fishing. Just then I spot Beckman and his friend trying to sneak out for some sort of rendezvous. "Not tonight," I yell over to him, and he gives me a dirty look. They exchange phone numbers, and we're on our way.

If there is an absolute queen of late-night drinking in Santa Cruz, it is Zona Lee Newbury of the Eastside Tavern on Soquel Avenue. She is the heavenly mother and patron saint of the well drink rolled into one. Her smile as we walk into the bar is downright infectious.

In recent years, the Eastside has developed a reputation as

a bikers' bar, a reputation no doubt fueled by the two-dozen Harleys that used to be parked outside. But they are long gone, for the most part, and besides, don't let the bikers scare you away. They're pussycats, really. "Big Bob," for instance, with his 3-foot chain, Bowie knife, boots and a scar from his forehead down to his chest, is actually a hairdresser in Soquel.

No longer does the Eastside sport a ping-pong table or a bookshelf that once included *On the Road,* but there are still two pool tables, a great shuffleboard, a dart game and pinball.

After Beckman beats me readily at 8-ball, an old timer in her 70s coaxes Beckman to dance to a Rolling Stones' tune. Dancing is prohibited here, but they break the rules momentarily anyway.

Zona Lee behind the bar never seems to lose her smile. "I've been tending bar here 10-and-a-half years," she says. "It's the people that keeps me coming back. We get a real cross-section here, people of all ages and backgrounds. In here, they're just people."

Over at the shuffleboard is Maralynn Dolphin, the bar's owner and *bon vivant* who's kept the place going through thick and thin. "The Eastside is a *bar* bar," she winks. "You've got your fern bars and your oyster bars and your this-and-that bars. Well, we're a *bar* bar, and there aren't too many of us left anymore."

After a quick drink at the Sportsman on Portola and the Hurry Back Inn on 41st, we stop in for some coffee at King's Court in Capitola, where the bartender, Donna, is the heir apparent to Zona Lee's throne. The Court has expanded these days, and now includes a dance floor with a DJ. But Donna breaks Beckman's heart by telling him she's gotten married, and we decide it's time for one last stop.

We descend down Wharf Road into Capitola Village and decide we have only one choice. Forget about those places where everyone looks like they just came out of an aerobics class. Mac's Patio is the jewel of the Esplanade.

Tucked into the far east corner of the village next to the Capitola Theater, Mac's is the perfect romantic hideaway, a throwback to the days when Bogie and Bacall drank hard and smoked hard and talked tough. If the bar has lost some of its original glitter over the years, it's retained all of its soul and charm.

A fire is glowing in the fireplace, and behind the electric piano bar is the one and only Jimmy Del Pierre, just as he has been five nights a week since 1978. There is no one quite like Jimmy, but if I had to make a comparison, I'd say he's something of a cross between Marty Robbins and one of the guitar players on the old Lawrence Welk Show. And he's smooth as good brandy.

As luck would have it, we are also graced by the presence of Dave Brown, who was a waiter at Mac's for over 15 years and who achieved notoriety of sorts when a local music critic mistakenly penned his obituary.

Brown is one of those sterling, unforgettable characters you encounter only a few times in life. He was a dancer on Broadway and in Las Vegas, and later had a brief career in Hollywood. Stricken by cancer a couple of years back, he was forced to quit his job and he has lost a good deal of his memory. But he has not lost his sense of humor nor his love of the nightlife.

Of the mistaken obituary, Brown saw only the irony in it, saying, "Man, it feels good to be alive." When I remind him that I first met him 17 years ago during a rocking Capitola storm, he looks at me and says, "My memory is gone, but I was bad, wasn't I? Oh, I had a good time." I remember how gracefully he waited tables at Mac's and danced at the Edgewater. I tell him he used to cut a mighty trim figure out there on the dance floor. "Yeah, man, I was bad," he smiles.*

Between Jimmy's songs I drop a dollar in his glass and ask him to play "Mona Lisa." Through the bar window I can see the lights dancing on the water and ghosts dancing there too.

---

*Dave Brown died of cancer on June 20, 1988

Beckman is falling asleep near the fire. I step outside for a moment and catch a little of that magic salt-sea air. As I stare up at the moon, I begin to see a familiar face and a soft smile.

Are you warm, are you real, Mona Lisa?
Or just a cold and lonely, lovely work of art?

—1988

FEAR AND LOATHING IN SANTA CRUZ

IT IS A LITTLE BEFORE 8:00 a.m., and already the Beach Flats neighborhood is abuzz with activity—women and men hurrying off to work, children playing at bus stops, old women sewing on porch steps. Smells pouring out of kitchens, rapid banter and Latin rhythms from the radio converge on the senses here beneath the early-morning shadows of the Boardwalk.

A late-model sedan turns left on Leibrandt Street and cruises slowly through the neighborhood. *"Migra!"* someone shouts. Suddenly the Flats are quiet again.

The sedan pulls over. An agent of the U.S. Border Patrol (*la migra*, in Spanish) emerges from the car and stops a young

Hispanic man on the sidewalk. The young man pulls some papers from his shirt pocket, shows them to the agent, who in turn looks them over carefully before he allows his detainee to proceed. This time, the agent returns to his car empty-handed.

Although generally hidden from the public eye, such scenes occur regularly in Santa Cruz County. "The *migra* creates a constant atmosphere of terror within the Hispanic community here," said a resident of Beach Flats. "Even people with green cards [resident visas] are afraid of them."

According to Bruce Haakedahl, the agent then in charge of the Border Patrol's Central California division, 4,328 undocumented workers were arrested in this region in 1984.

Just how many of those arrests took place specifically in Santa Cruz, Haakedahl couldn't say, though he did indicate the number was "significant."

Border Patrol agents make daily scans of the Santa Cruz County Jail, according to Haakedahl, and also wind up at local job sites following tips from employers. Haakedahl further acknowledges that the Border Patrol receives tips on the whereabouts of illegal aliens from the Santa Cruz Police Department. "We often get calls from police agencies, particularly when there is suspicion of criminal activity."

In the fall of 1979, then-U.S. Attorney General Benjamin Civiletti ordered a halt to Border Patrol sweeps of residential neighborhoods and limited agent activity in such areas only when there was "probable cause" to believe that an alien might be living at a specific address. A tip from a local police agency provides Border Patrol agents with "probable cause" protection—and allows them to enter the neighborhoods.

Four agents working out of a central office in Salinas are responsible for patrolling all of Santa Cruz and Monterey Counties, in addition to portions of Santa Clara and San Benito counties. "Obviously, we don't have the adequate power to patrol this vast region," Haakedahl complained. "We have a pretty impossible task."

Known as the "enforcement arm" of the U.S. Immigration and Naturalization Service (INS), the Border Patrol was founded in 1924—and it has long been used as a political tool by government agencies and big business.

U.S. presidents since Calvin Coolidge have often stepped up Border Patrol activity to divert public attention from unemployment and failed economic policies by creating an atmosphere of xenophobia.

Such was the case when President Reagan ordered a Border Patrol operation in 1982 known as "Project Jobs," a weeklong sweep of nine metropolitan areas intended to produce employment for domestic workers and which resulted in the arrests of fewer than 6,000 undocumented workers nationwide. There was all but unanimous agreement on the part of economic experts that the multi-million dollar project had had virtually no impact on the unemployment rate.

No one knows for certain how many undocumented workers are employed in Santa Cruz County. "I couldn't begin to make an estimate," said Haakedahl. "I can only go by the facts—the number of those we arrest."

In a report released in 1983 by the Center for U.S.-Mexican Studies in San Diego, Leo R. Chavez and associates estimated that there are 85,000 illegal aliens working in the greater San Francisco Bay Area. The vast majority of them, according to Chavez, were employed at extremely low wages in agriculture, the electronics and garment industries, restaurants and hotels.

"U.S. born workers," said Chavez, "have indicated that they are not interested in such employment."

Chavez also dispelled the popular myth that Mexican immigrants are a drain on state and federal welfare programs. "The 1980 U.S. Select Commission on Immigration and Refugee Policy," Chavez said, "found no large amount of utilization of taxpayer-funded services." Chavez said that he had no reason to believe that Santa Cruz County provided an exception to these findings.

Border Patrol agent Haakedahl refrained from discussing

the political and economic implications of his agency. "Our mission is to arrest those aliens who are living and working in this country illegally. That's the law."

There are those, however, who argue that the Border Patrol is selective in its enforcement of the legal code. The U.S. economy, they propose, is dependent upon a high level of cheap, foreign labor, and Border Patrol activity often coincides with the needs of employers.

"During harvest time, the *migra* is never around," said a Watsonville resident and former member of the United Farm Workers' Union. "Once the season is over, the growers don't need us until next year—and the *migra* gets busy again."

—1984

SOLDIERS OF THE CROSS

SEVENTY-YEAR-OLD EDITH MANCHESTER has the meticulous look of a prim-and-proper English schoolmarm. Bespectacled and with her long, gray hair pulled back into a bun, Manchester would be indistinguishable from any other Santa Cruz grandmother were it not for the two little gold feet pinned to her button-down blouse. The feet have become her trademark and, as she notes with a challenging grin, they are not to be confused with the insignia of Hang Ten beach wear. "This little pro-life pin represents the feet of the unborn child," she declares in a holier-than-thou tone, "thousands of whom are being murdered in this country every day. You know, after just eight weeks, the human fetus has legs and arms with perfectly formed feet and hands. Abortion, quite simply, is the killing of a human being."

Give Edith Manchester a soapbox and she'll jump onto it. In addition to abortion, she's equally comfortable condemning sex education in the schools, the Equal Rights Amendment, homosexuality, the American Civil Liberties Union, Nicaragua, godless communism, godless feminism, and heaven forbid, even the now-godless Santa Cruz *Sentinel.* In fact, there isn't a whole lot in contemporary American society, save for Ronald Reagan, with which she finds herself at ease. "The United States Constitution has been deliberately twisted by a group of secular humanists with a socialist agenda. They're against all individual rights—property rights, parents' rights, free enterprise—and they're against God. It started with the New Deal and it's been going on full-flower since the 1960s."

Raised by missionary parents in China during the era of Sun Yat-sen, Manchester grew up with a peculiarly American sense of Christian duty. At the age of 17, she returned to the States to study music at Wellesley College and later attended graduate school at Harvard. In 1942, she moved to California, where she married and eventually raised 12 children. All the while, she has been a good Christian soldier. "The only source of power in life is Jesus Christ," says the articulate, genuinely affable Manchester, "and his power is giving you the power of God."

To dismiss Manchester as but another harmless, Bible-toting extremist is to bury one's head in the sand. Although her name rarely appears in headlines, Manchester's views of the world have affected the lives of thousands of women, children and men in Santa Cruz County. She has served as area president of the city's Parent-Teachers Association, in addition to heading the PTAs at Soquel High, Del Mar Middle, and Branciforte Junior High schools. She was active in the successful 1978 campaign to recall progressive supervisor Phil Baldwin (whom, in the spirit of Joe McCarthy, she labeled a socialist), and she remains a persistent critic of local progressives in the letters columns of area newspapers. More recently, Manchester has focused her so-called Christian activism on Planned Parenthood, local abortion clinics, and sex-education programs in the public schools; according to her critics, however, many of these activities have been almost vicious and, for that matter, decidedly un-Christian. And perhaps more important, Edith Manchester is no longer acting alone.

Today, Manchester is President of the Santa Cruz County Christian Action Council (CAC), a local chapter of the national anti-abortion organization founded by evangelist Billy Graham in 1975 and a spearhead of the religious right movement in the United States. CAC's stated purpose is "solving the abortion problem through the application of Biblical truths." The CAC actively calls upon our legislators "to bring this nation's laws into harmony with God's Law," which teaches "Thou shalt not kill." While most of the CAC's national energies are centered on the attempt to reverse the landmark 1973 *Roe v. Wade* Supreme Court decision which established a woman's constitutional right to abortion, the majority of CAC's local chapters have spearheaded campaigns against Planned Parenthood and local abortion clinics. The Santa Cruz chapter— which, according to Manchester, claims well over 100 dues-paying members—has proved to be no exception.

Manchester founded the Santa Cruz CAC in January 1983, and one of the organization's first acts was to take out anti-abortion advertisements in the Santa Cruz *Sentinel, Good Times*, and the now-defunct *Express*. These ads produced an outcry from Santa Cruz pro-choice advocates, who the following week took out ads of their own. Cynthia Matthews, Director of Public Affairs for Planned Parenthood, stated during the time of the controversy, "Our philosophy is one of personal decision. We don't have a preconceived idea of what to do in crisis situations...If I were a young woman involved in an unwanted pregnancy, I definitely would have been scared to death by the [CAC] ad."

Soon thereafter, CAC members began picketing local abortion clinics, an activity which continues to this day. While Manchester refers to the picketing as "sidewalk counseling," those on the other side term it harassment. Carrying signs which read "Abortion is Murder" and "Babies Die by Choice," the picketers frequently approach women who are entering the centers. In January of 1986, after protesters chanted anti-abortion slogans through the morning at Choice Medical Group on Mission Drive, the Sheriff's Department was called in and CAC members were ordered to halt their encounters with Choice clients. According to witnesses, one young woman broke into tears when a Christian protester yelled at her, "They'll kill your baby in there. It's murder for profit."

When Planned Parenthood began performing abortions, that organization also became a weekly target for picketers, sometimes numbering as many as 40. Many of the scenes which ensued outside were far from pretty. "During one picket here," said Planned Parenthood Executive Director Michael Hall, "a very angry young man really scared me. A woman from the neighborhood came to him and said that she was concerned about the fact that her three-year-old son had found a CAC pamphlet; it had grotesque babies-in-the-garbage-can photos—which probably were of stillbirths.

"She said to him, 'You've scared my baby' and 'he's too young to understand.' She was also upset and crying. Then this CAC guy started in on her with the whole babies-are-being-murdered line and had no compassion for the woman or her child. She got more upset and the guy kept spouting rhetoric. When I tried to intervene, he yelled that I had thousands of babies' blood on my hands and said that on the day of judgment, God would punish me...When I see people as angry as this guy was, I get frightened, because that is where violence comes from."

Manchester, however, doesn't see how such incidents can be called harassment. "We really don't yell at anyone," she says. "We merely come up to the women and offer them our literature and the truth of God. Admittedly, our presence makes many people uncomfortable, but it's only because they already have a guilty conscience. They're the ones who are abusing human life—we're not."

When asked if adding to one's difficulties at a time of crisis is truly reflective of the Christian spirit, Manchester nods her head in affirmation. "We offer them a way out: adoption referral, financial help, spiritual counseling, job training, any kind of service that they need. That's the Christian response to a crisis pregnancy."

Planned Parenthood's Hall disagrees. "Edith Manchester says things that are patently dishonest," he contends. "The whole movement is very untruthful. It never ceases to amaze me how ironic it is, calling them Christian. The means to their ends are unconscionable."

Dr. William Levonian, a prominent Santa Cruz family practitioner, also believes that there are no excuses for abortion, though his rhetoric is more scientific than ecumenical. The father of five children (two of them adopted), Levonian is regional vice-president of the California Pro-Life Medical Association, and his wife, Nancy, is co-director of Birthright, a local anti-abortion counseling center.

"I don't really see abortion as having anything to do with religion," says Levonian in the living room of his plush Prospect Heights home. "Even people who haven't given it much thought will see that when doctors are saving premature babies in one wing of the hospital that are younger than the babies they're destroying in another wing, then something's not right. Medicine keeps moving the viability of life farther and farther back, supporting the fact that abortion is the killing of a live human being and must stop." A mother has no "right" to kill a fetus, he adds, because both are human beings and have equal right to life. "You see that picture of my adopted teenage daughter. If she had been conceived in this era, she would have been destroyed."

A Congregationalist Christian, Levonian has a great deal of admiration for the fundamentalists leading the anti-abortion cause. "They are much like the original Christians. They would almost be willing to go to their deaths to fulfill what they feel is right. Those are worthy people, more worthy than I. It's hard to find people that decent. I wish my religious feelings were as strong as theirs."

Levonian, nonetheless, stresses that he is not a member of any local group of anti-abortion activists. He prefers to work independently, writing letters, lecturing to groups such as the Knights of Columbus, testifying before state commissions, introducing resolutions before the California Medical Association, and writing articles for medical magazines. There is a certain shrewdness in Levonian's use of scientific, rather than religious, arguments against abortion. In public, he represents the more rational side of the anti-abortion movement. In private, however, he acknowledges that he wants his "behavior to reflect what Christ wants me to do."

While Levonian is not a member of the Christian Action Council, he has joined other CAC members in attacking another of the religious right's pet peeves, sex-education programs in the public schools. Levonian was outraged when he learned a few years ago that his daughter visited Planned Parenthood with her classmates on an 11th grade field trip. He had signed a permission slip for field trips, but wasn't told where the class was going. "You don't want to send your children to school and find that your teaching at home is being undermined as if you're the enemy. That's wrong. No parent likes that."

In 1982 a group calling itself the "Women's Committee for Responsible Government" (a misnomer if there ever was one, given the fact that the committee is made up mostly of men, including Levonian) filed suit against the California State Office of Family Planning and the state departments of Health Services and Education. The suit accused the state of "promoting abortion and radical sexual philosophy and the religion of secular humanism." Still pending, the suit seeks a court order to prohibit funding for any such curricula and could alter the way public schools teach children about sex.

The focus of the suit is a 1976 statewide teacher's guide that was developed by the local Planned Parenthood. While the guide is fairly straightforward in its approach to sex education, the Women's Committee objects to the guide's failure to promote sexual abstinence to the exclusion of all other practices for minors. The WCRG also finds the guide to be "weighted in favor of feminism, masturbation, homosexuality, abortion, the elimination of sex roles and adolescent sexual behavior as long as it is effectively contracepted."

According to the committee, "The manual reinforces the State's propaganda that there are no absolute moral standards or right answers in the areas of sex, family life, morality and religion," which is commonly referred to as "secular humanism" by the religious right.

Planned Parenthood's Hall calls the WCRG action a nuisance suit and stresses that a variety of community members were involved in developing all of the school curricula in question. "Planned Parenthood believes that informed people can make the best decision for themselves," Hall continued. "We seek to respect a plurality of different views on sexuality depending on different people. Our tolerance isn't respected by the Christian right, however; they want others to live their lives the way they do themselves."

As Hall's Planned Parenthood colleague, Matthews, pointed out, "For years the moralists of the new religious right have argued that access to sex education and family planning have the effect of encouraging teens to be sexually active, thus being responsible for teen pregnancy. On the contrary, a recent study from Johns Hopkins University shows that comprehensive sexuality education programs actually result in later sexual activity for teen girls and reduce the incidence of teen pregnancy."

The present Deukmejian administration, however, appears to be caving in to the demands of Christians state wide. It has met with WCRG members over settlement of the sex-education suit and gives all indication that it will reach a compromise on sex-education funding. Deukmejian even offered to fund a pro-abstinence film as part of a sex-education compromise, but the WCRG declined and remained firm in its goal of eliminating all sex education that offers abstinence only as one of many possible pregnancy preventions.

If the pending WCRG lawsuit is successful, it will mark the third time this year that the religious right has pushed back California educational policy on family planning. In the spring of 1987 Deukmejian appointees used unfounded charges of "racial stereotyping" as an excuse to cancel funding for a video to be produced by none other than Planned Parenthood of Santa Cruz. A dramatization of a teenage girl's conflict around an unwanted pregnancy, written by award-winning Santa Cruz filmmaker Eric Thiermann, the film would have been the first by Planned Parenthood designed specifically for the Hispanic community. Another film by a San Francisco filmmaker was also axed following roars of discontent from the religious right. "Sex education is destroying our young people," says Manchester succinctly, as if she's said it more than a few times before. "It's ruining our schools, and it's ruining our society. Abstinence is the only method that's tolerable in God's eyes."

Five miles up Highway 17 in the little silicon suburb of Scotts Valley, the Christian right has made even greater headway into the body politic than in neighboring Santa Cruz. The Reverend Glennon Culwell, pastor of the Scotts Valley First Baptist Church for nearly three decades, was elected to the Scotts Valley City Council in June of 1987 in what some observers called one of the dirtiest political campaigns in Santa Cruz County history.

Barbara Leichter, a moderate liberal, was one of the council candidates defeated by Culwell and conservative Phil Liberty. It is Leichter's view that large sums of money were channeled into Scotts Valley from sources outside the city in order to influence the election. Yet money wasn't what made the Scotts Valley campaign dirty. It was the tactics used by Culwell and his supporters. The day before the election, dozens of children and students from nearby Bethany Bible College gathered at a freeway overpass to display Culwell and Liberty signs. According to Leichter, many of the picketers harassed her and her daughter while they were out campaigning, calling them "communist pigs," "sluts" and other derogatory names. There were charges that votes were being bought and the young Culwell supporters were being paid up to $10 an hour and pressured by their churches for their support.

Leichter says that "two years ago religion didn't have a place in political campaigns. This year, as I was going door to door, I was frequently asked if I was a Christian. When I told people I was Jewish, they asked if I was a 'complete Jew,' if I had accepted Christ as my savior."

Although this was his first foray into electoral politics, Culwell has been preaching conservative political views from the pulpit for 27 years, condemning just about everything from rock music to communism. Locals remember him for his crusade against the Hip Pocket Bookstore on Pacific Avenue, a 1960s counterculture spot which carried what Culwell characterized as "salacious" books and magazines. In the heyday of Santa Cruz acid rock, he was an ardent critic of rock and roll and fought to shut down The Barn, a Scotts Valley nightclub frequented by the likes of Janis Joplin, Led Zepplin, and Ken Keysey's Merry Pranksters.

In 1987, Culwell attempted to pass a resolution which would have had local church leaders pray at the opening of each council meeting. The resolution was barely defeated by a split two-two vote with one abstention, and Culwell was upset by the defeat. "We're afraid to let the public know that we're calling on the Creator [for guidance]."

The constitutional distinctions between church and state are ones which most of the religious right would rather ignore.

"I believe that God is in control of our lives," says Manchester, "not just at Sunday church services. God wants good government."

"The Constitution doesn't guarantee us freedom from religion, but freedom of religion," she continues. "The Supreme Court rulings which have reified the separation of church and state in the last 40 years have twisted the intent of those who founded this country."

Yet while the religious right feels quite comfortable with merging politics and religion, ironically it doesn't feel nearly as comfortable mixing politics with Christian charity. Culwell, for instance, declared that he won't allow government money, including federal revenue sharing funds, to be spent on child care centers and senior programs. "I will not take your dollars to invest in social programs," he promised taxpayers last June. "You invest them and get the credit." While building roads and protecting property are the duties of the government, helping human beings in need, according to the Christian right, is not.

Generally, Culwell is pleased by the role the religious right has taken in national and local politics. "Christians should exert as much influence as they can," he says. "If we're excluded from politics, then we're excluded from a main area of life."*

—1987

*Written with Bill Hall. In February 1989, Culwell received an unsigned, off-color Valentine from Santa Cruz City Council member Mo Reich, an act which subsequently led to Reich's resignation from the Council.

HAPPINESS IS AN ITALIAN MAMA

My mother and I are of decidedly different generations and mind sets. A self-described "plenty-nine-years" young, she is a pristine product of that era which came of age during the Second World War and which continues to celebrate itself in the Reagan presidency. Her current heroines are the president's wife, Nancy, and Blanche, Dorothy and Rose on TV's *Golden Girls*.

The daughter of turn-of-the-century immigrant parents, she still sees the world in terms of Italian proverbs and Catholic mysticism. For every problem in life, there is an appropriate proverb—and for every proverb, there is another one. She gets all the news she needs from the National Enquirer, Rona Barret and her hairdresser at Verna's Salon. Paul Harvey is too liberal for her. Needless to say, we disagree on just about anything and everything, and generally we have a wonderful time doing so.

In contrast to what I view as my mother's cultural and

political naiveté, I fancy myself a street-wise intellectual, schooled in both the Ivy League and the tenderloin, incapable of being fooled or outsmarted by anyone, including myself. My mother, however, knows better and from time to time she lets me know it, too.

Given our differences, one might expect that she and I would keep our distance from each other, if not so much to keep peace, then at least to maintain our sanity. Not so. Italian mothers love their sons, and vice versa. Unlike most Americans, we both still live in the same community in which we were raised, and I tend a productive vegetable garden in a plot just next to her home. We see each other almost daily, vehemently addressing our various points of contention over ravioli, coffee, biscotti or a little red wine. If it's bad for the blood pressure, it's good for the soul. When I leave, she tells me to go get a haircut, then raids my garden for tomatoes and sweet basil.

I think it is fair to say that I win most of our skirmishes over issues of the day. It is also rather difficult to win bets which place El Salvador in South America, but geography was never her strong suit. She is a gracious loser, I must add, since bringing more of her homemade cookies to the table is certainly a sign of grace.

For all the attention my mother pays to the latest fashion trends and Elizabeth Taylor's love triangles, she is nonetheless one of the most perceptive people I know when it gets down to the nuts and bolts of life. She is one savvy woman, as they say, full of the most profound insights which are usually rendered at the most opportune of times. Let me offer a couple of examples.

Some time ago she was fluttering about the kitchen, seemingly oblivious to me as I nursed a beer and buried my head in the sports pages. There was something nagging me at the time, a not-so-subtle ruffle in my life that was yanking at my stomach and the back of my neck. I wasn't sure what it was and definitely hadn't said a word about it to my mother.

In the middle of chopping some onions, she looked over at

me and said, "You're trying to do too many things, honey. You need a little more focus in your life. Cut off some of those loose edges."

"*Giorno per giorno*," she added, which loosely means "take it one day at a time."

I was startled by her observation, coming as it did completely out of the blue, though I wasn't surprised. She had picked up on my psychic turmoil before and, of course, she was right once again. I did need focus. The loose ends were nagging at me. The diagnosis and prescription were as accurate as they could be.

A few years earlier, the stakes had been much greater. A rotten romance and a motorcycle accident had brought me to the edge of self-destruction. I was laid up in bed, emotionally as well as physically broken, ready to call this lousy game quits. One afternoon my mother walked into my room, sat down next to me, and quietly listened to the desperate melancholia I was spewing forth at great abundance.

When I finished, she talked very quietly about tragedies she had suffered in her own life—tragedies that made my own dime-store drama seem very tame. She then conveyed to me her simple solution for overcoming them. "Look to the beauty in life," she said, and she said it in such a way that I knew it had to be true. It was.

All of this leads me to conclude that we should never underestimate the power of our mothers. At a time today when many men are following the path of the poet Robert Bly and are seeking rapprochements with their fathers, I say do so cautiously and without severing ties with your mothers. The potential dangers are many and ominous. There are many things which only a mother can know and which only they can help us heal. They represent our connection to the earth and to both the mysteries and wisdom of life. Do nothing to diminish it.

—1987

LEMON DROPS

WHEN MY COUSINS AND I were young, my great-aunt Josie would chase us with a beat-up old broom to keep us from her garden. With her arms cocked high above her head and her body shaking with anger, she would curse us in Italian and broken English, calling us little shits and devils. Though she was tiny and seemed terribly old, her eyes were still fierce and her hands were still strong enough so that we did not laugh at her until we had found refuge a block or so away.

As Josie scuttled back to working in the soil, we would shout out taunts at her, giggling and laughing, no doubt secretly terrified by the fierceness of her attacks. We even had a song we sang about her, our own bastardization of that playground favorite:

> *Whistle while you work,*
> *Josie is a jerk,*
> *Josephina bit her wiener*
> *Now it doesn't work.*

We called her a witch and worse. Sometimes we made her cry.

My great-aunt's full name was Josephina Angelina Loero. Along with her family, she arrived in Santa Cruz from San Francisco as an infant in the immediate aftermath of the 1906 earthquake, and she lived on the corner of Gharkey and Laguna Streets the rest of her life. In the early 1960s, when extended families had all but disappeared in America, her eldest sister, Battistina, lived next door with her family, while another sister, Clara, lived with her brood less than half a block away. Assorted nieces and nephews also lived nearby.

Josie spent a good deal of time in the basement of her home, which she had inherited from her mother, Celestina, who died at the age of 94. It was dark in there and filled with the smells of garlic, onions, basil, rosemary and other herbs drying on the rafters. There were old family portraits hanging on the walls, and Josie's garden tools and baskets filled with beans and tomatoes. I remember always being a little scared to go in there and never liked going alone. I was certain it was haunted, and was afraid that bats might be living there as well. Once, I was sure I heard the ghost of my great-grandmother lurking in the shadows.

It was an eerie place all right, but its one salvation was a stash of lemon drop candy which Josie always kept there and which she distributed regularly, as long as we stayed out of her garden.

I loved those little candies. I relished their roughness of texture when you first placed them in your mouth, the rush of sweetness from the sugar coating, and the bitter bite of the hard yellow candy that followed. Whenever I was in the mood for one, I would gather my courage and venture over to Josie's, waiting for her offer. She rarely let me down.

Although you will not read about my great-aunt in any of the many history books written about Santa Cruz, nor find her honored by any of the local historical societies, she was certainly a remarkable woman, a fiercely independent woman, with her own rather fascinating story.

It seems, among other things, that my great-aunt was famous for her onions. Once, a few years ago as I was tending my own crop of Italian reds, an older cousin of mine politely informed me that they would never be as big as Josie's. "She once grew a 13-and-a-half pounder," he said. Somewhere in the back of my mind I recalled this legend and was forced to face the fact that my onions would never match up to hers.

Hyperbole is something of a family trait (and exaggeration to go along with it), and a farmer friend of mine later explained to me that a 13-and-a-half pound onion would be rather close to an impossibility, unless it were the size of a watermelon. Nonetheless, a few months ago as I was rummaging through some family photos, I came across a faded newspaper clipping from the Santa Cruz *Sentinel* which, lo and behold, heralded the miracle of Josie's onions.

"Giant Onions are Harvested at Laguna Street," the article was captioned, and it went on to note that "vegetables grow big and luscious in the garden of Josephine Loero. Her success formula is simple. She keeps the ground free of weeds and loose around the plants. She waters the vegetables once a week, letting the water run slowly into deep ditches between the rows, so that it will soak down to the roots." There was a picture of her smiling, wearing her best cotton dress. And the onion she was holding was very big indeed. Perhaps two or three pounds.

In addition to her gardening exploits, my great-aunt was also a notorious wine drinker. This I can confirm on my own, as I vividly recall the bitter, musty smell of her breath and her frequent visits to the demijohn in her home. One of my uncles tells the story of the time Josie was missing for dinner. "Where's Josie?" everyone kept asking, but she wasn't to be found.

The family looked all over for her, until someone finally decided to search the wine cellar (it was Josie, after all). There she lay, according to the legend, passed out on the floor, her head resting just below the spigot from the wine barrel, looking quite content in the dark red puddle.

Much to my surprise, I heard this very same story repeated in my family's home town in Italy when I traveled there a few years ago. Although Josie had never journeyed to the homeland (I'm sure she never had the money), her legend had, in the form of this story: "You are of the people that drinks wine," my cousin in Italy would jest in reference to Josie's habit. I laughed at the time, but it seems sad to me now, almost tragic. What a great pain she must have carried.

Long after Josie died, I learned that she had been married once, though only for a day. The marriage had been arranged, which was the Italian practice of the time, and a date set, though Josie didn't have a whole lot of say in the matter. The prospective groom, an Italian immigrant from San Francisco, came to Santa Cruz for the wedding, and the newlyweds were to make their home in the city.

The wedding photo is a marvelous portrait of gloom, particularly Josie's. She looks anything but happy. There she is in her white gown and veil, her constricted body language revealing her distaste for the whole affair. When the wedding was over, she and her new husband made their way down to the Union Pacific Depot on Washington Street to await the train that would take them to San Francisco. The children of the Italian neighborhood, many of them Josie's nieces and nephews and distant cousins, followed the couple along the way, teasing Josie and singing songs, much like we would 40 years later. Apparently, one of her wedding shoes was lost in a gopher hole beside the trail, so she had to make the remainder of the journey with one bare foot.

According to my mother, who was a flower girl in the wedding (and who can be seen smirking in the photo), Josie returned home shortly thereafter. It seems as though there were a few details about married life that no one had explained to Josie, particularly pertaining to a certain part of the male anatomy, and she did not take favorably to them. Upon her return, Josie was sullen but unbowed, and she resumed her life of gardening, mending fishing nets, picking Brussels sprouts up the coast, and working in the canneries. No one ever arranged for her to marry again.

By the time my generation rolled around, Josie appeared to be decidedly out of place in a world of spaceships, television, electric can openers and sports cars. She never seemed to be part of the modern world. In fact, she was mostly oblivious to it, and she went about her daily routine as the women in Italy 8,000 miles away had done for centuries. There is no doubt she would have been more at home there.

My last memory of Josie is of driving her and my grandmother and my aunt to the old Catholic cemetery off Capitola Road. I was in high school at the time, with a beat-up 1960 Ford Falcon, and the four of us piled in to go pay our respects to the dead. In all honesty, I remember being a little embarrassed about having them in the car and was worried what my friends would think if they saw me with these three, rather odd old ladies, on our way to the cemetery, no less. Such a fool. What I wouldn't give to have the three of them back with me now.

In spite of my social reservations, however, I actually enjoyed having them in the car and listening to them banter and argue in the old Italian dialect. It was rich and warm and musical. I'd tell them to be quiet, and my grandmother would shake her fist at me and tap me on the chin.

When we arrived at the cemetery, with its marbled mausoleums and cold gray tombstones, they would go through a ritual of discarding the old flowers and water from the brass vases, wipe them clean, arrange the fresh flowers, and then fill them to the brim with clean water. I can still remember the rancid smell of the old flowers. Always, the women would cry loudly and endlessly, but this time I noticed that Josie seemed quieter than usual, sullen, reserved. Perhaps she saw her own death in the soft reflections of the white marble. Maybe she even wished for it and the quiet peace it would bring.

When I left them all off and suffered through their hugs and kisses, Josie reached into her pocket and handed me a lemon drop. It was the last time I would ever see her.

I put the candy in my mouth and sucked hard on it. As always, it was bittersweet—bittersweet like Josie's life, often lonely and sad, but with enough good wine and big red onions to make it all seem bearable.

—1988

FIRST STEPS, FINAL THOUGHTS

MY NINE-YEAR-OLD DAUGHTER is presently dancing in and out with the waves at Cowell's Beach, just to the west side of the Santa Cruz wharf. It is a bright, if somewhat chilled, late winter afternoon, and the sun is sparkling on the water like a shattered mirror. Across the bay the Monterey peninsula looms like a distant island—dark, alluring, Oz-like. More immediate is little Neary Creek, a few yards to my right, which tumbles virtually unnoticed through the city, emerges from a one-foot steel pipe beneath Beach Street, and carves a slinky "S" through the sand on its way into the bay.

My daughter is running back and forth at the meeting place of these two divergent waterways, this magical aquatic juncture where one way of life begins and another ends. Suddenly she squats, reaches into the sand and squeals with delight. She jumps to her feet, scurries up the berm, and places a squiggly little sand crab at my feet. With a ballerina spin and a series of happy cartwheels, she is back down at the water. A trio of sea gulls scatters as she approaches, their wing spans appearing longer than she. My heart is about ready to burst.

If there is one place on earth, one single spot on this madly spinning planet which beckons to me, which calls out to me like a Don Juan *sitio*, it is here. This is where my roots to this town, this world and this universe begin.

Well over a century and two decades ago, an audacious 14-year-old Italian sailor jumped ship on the old Cowell railroad wharf, hooked up with some Spanish fish peddlers, and decided to call Santa Cruz his home. This was the first place he ever stepped foot on in America. That young boy was my great grandfather, and years later, in 1914, at the grand opening of the present wharf, a photographer set him down for a photo session with his fishing nets and some family members he helped to bring here from Italy. Three-quarters of a century later, I am sitting in the very same spot, which now stretches back and forth in time to link five generations. It's hard not to get nostalgic.

Indeed, much of my family's history runs awfully close to this little mound of sand. Since the day the wharf first opened 75 years ago, my kinfolk have spent the better part of their lives toiling on its craggy wooden frame and on the west side cliffs which overlook it. My own parents met just down the beach a summertime long ago, and I spent my childhood here with my cousins, all of us frolicking in the surf on rubber mats that we pumped up daily at Otto's gas station across the street. That was long before the Dream Inn would come to cast its dark shadow over the beach. We would buy ten-cent juice bars at a long-forgotten snack stand and slurp them up while we lay in the sand with our backs to the sun. Our moms always stayed on the other side of the pier, but we liked it better over here, away from parental earshot and where, to our judgment anyway, the waves always seemed a little bigger and better for riding.

Those were truly the best of times. Imagine Santa Cruz one-fifth the size it is today, with a look that my friend Morton Marcus once described as having "that rough edge"—"faded gingerbread Victorian mansions" mixed with "cracked stucco bungalows or white clapboard cottages like overturned life-boats emerging from the fog." The county, he observed, was "a well-worn rosary of small towns that had been rubbed too long, too hard, between the fingers of fog and wind, sunlight and rain." There was none of the generic suburban sprawl which defines new construction today. The bay was full of fish and fishermen, and you could catch halibut and jack smelt and ling cod right off the wharf.

One of my most vivid summertime memories from that era is of my grandmother, Batistina, arriving at the wharf each day around noon in the passenger side of an old fish truck. She would have whomever was driving her slow down so that she could wave to us on the beach. She worked on the wharf well into the spring of her 84th year, when one night after closing time, she rested her head on a dinner table she was cleaning and passed away. This is where I came to cry the following day, my tears leaving tiny droplets in the sand.

So much has changed since then. Had a modern-day Rip Van Winkle gone to sleep twenty years ago, he would no doubt be stunned by the political shifts Santa Cruz has encumbered in recent years, the incessant growth, the traffic and conges-tion. There have been many times lately when I tire of all the changes and the city's constant political turmoil, the perennial tug-of-war between those of the old-time Santa Cruz (whose partisans, ironically, continue to push for growth and change) and those of the new Santa Cruz who arrived largely with the university (and who, with equal irony, oppose growth and change, except, of course, when it takes place on the hill). Linked by history and by blood to one, and by education and politics to the other, I often feel internally torn by the perpet-

171

ual tension between the two, so much so that at this moment I am wont to say: A plague on both your houses.

That, however, is a fancy which soon passes, for as I look out at the magnificent panorama of bay and coastline before me, I know full well that my vista would most definitely include oil platforms and convention centers and a plethora of high-rise hotels, were it not for the political and environmental battles which have been waged—and won—in the government centers uptown.

But I diverge. Out in the water, politics and familial history have little meaning to the young girl with the flowing blonde hair who is now calling for her daddy to come play with her. The Ohlone Indians who first inhabited this piece of earth had a song they sang about "dancing on the brink of the world." As I watch my daughter swaying with the waves and wind, I have a feeling that she is doing just that. Again she calls out to her daddy.

The water against her skin is so cold that it stings when she jumps up into my arms and asks me to carry her out into the water beyond the breakers. I can feel her tiny little heart beating wildly to keep her warm. I look down the beach both ways. We are the only humans out in the water for as far as the eye can see. We have this whole wonderful world to ourselves.

The view from out here is utterly familiar. It strikes me that I have lived all but a few months of my life between Lighthouse Point and the cement ship in Seacliff to the south, and for a second I feel almost claustrophobic. On our way through the breakers, I suggest that now might be a good time to move away from Santa Cruz to another town where there aren't so many people and so many controversies. "No way, daddy," my daughter says emphatically as a wave crashes against my upper torso. "This is where all my friends and family live. I love it here."

I am surprised by both the strength of her conviction and her developed sense of place. Her feelings are not rooted in the past, but in the future, and she has forced me to look forward, not behind. "O.K.," I tell her, proud that she has taken a stand. "We'll stay."

The coldness of the water accentuates her concern. She hangs on tightly as we move farther from shore. Without knowing it, she has just taken her first real step in Santa Cruz, much like her great-great-grandfather 120 years ago; she has claimed it as her own. And also without knowing it, she has just concurred with him, too: This is a fine place to live. Family and friends do matter. This is home.

—1989